Merchandising the Anointing
Developing Discernment
For These Last Days

Merchandising the Anointing
Developing Discernment
For These Last Days

Rick Renner

Rick Renner Ministries
P. O. Box 1709
Tulsa, Oklahoma 74101

Unless otherwise indicated, all Scripture quotations are taken from the *King James Version* of the Bible.

Merchandising the Anointing
Developing Discernment For These Last Days
ISBN 1-88008-908-4
Copyright © 1990 by Rick Renner Ministries
P. O. Box 1709
Tulsa, Oklahoma 74101

Published by ALBURY PUBLISHING
P. O. Box 740406
Tulsa, Oklahoma 74147-0406

2nd Printing

Dedication

I want to dedicate this book to my three wonderful sons, Paul, Philip and Joel.

Thank you, boys, for understanding that Dad is called to be a man of God; thank you for praying for Daddy so faithfully; thank you for being right in there with us in the work of the Lord; involving yourselves in our ministry and for expressing your love for others; and thank you most of all for being the children that you are to your mother and me.

Table of Contents

Acknowledgements

I want to personally thank all those friends and acquaintances who took the time to read the rough manuscript of this new book and to keep me in prayer as I was writing it.

First of all, I must thank my wonderful wife, Denise, for her loving, thoughtful and helpful suggestions as I sought God during this project. Your comments meant more to me than any one else's.

Second, I want to thank the many notable leaders who responded to my request and took time out of their busy schedules to read the rough manuscript of this book. I also want to thank you for giving me your encouraging, candid comments, and honest and straightforward suggestions. Thank you so very, very much.

I also want to thank my pastor friends across the nation and those advisory board members of Rick Renner Ministries, who also took time out of their schedules to read the original manuscript of this book and for keeping me in prayer as I was writing.

And last, I must say thank you so very much to my wonderful staff for their relentless work and prayer. Specifically, I wish to thank Louise Norcom for her tremendous editorial work; and to Jennifer Bolding and Beth Parker for their helpful suggestions in regard to the original manuscript.

Chapter 1
The Perfect Example of the False Prophet Problem

I will never forget the day when a well-known and respectable minister friend informed me of a terribly detestable event that had occurred at a large Christian gathering in our city.

As he related the story to me, I could hardly believe what my ears were hearing. This was the most blatant, outrageous case of fraud in the pulpit that I had heard of in years. Disgust, horror and a sickening feeling came over me as he told me that a false prophet was in the camp.

Prior to this conversation with my friend, I always had strange feelings about the minister in question. However, because of her growing popularity and widespread acceptance among many spiritual leaders, I had conceded to keep my questions and suspicions to myself. I had hoped that my suspicions were wrong.

It is true that she seemed to have supernatural activity in her meetings. However, I was greatly distressed by some of her strange, supernatural manifestations that could not be substantiated by the Word of God. The bleeding from her hands, feet, side, back and forehead, and the thick oil that oozed from her hands and feet, as far as I could tell, had no precedent in scripture.

She claimed the oil was a supernatural manifestation of the "oil of the Holy Spirit." From time to time, this oil oozed out of her hands and feet so much, that puddles would begin gathering on the floor around the places where she had been sitting or standing during her services.

Though the scriptures never applied, she attempted to substantiate this "sign and wonder" from the Word. She quoted from Acts 2:19, which says, "I will show wonders in the heavens above, and signs in the earth beneath; blood, and fire, and vapour of smoke."

On the basis of this scripture, she declared that this blood and oil was a supernatural sign and wonder from God that testified to the blood of Jesus and the supernatural work of the Holy Spirit.

In one meeting, she even allegedly stated that she was just so full of God that she simply couldn't contain it all — it just had to come out in "liquid form!"

Isn't it odd that the Lord Jesus, Paul, Peter, James or John didn't have this problem? These men were so full of God that genuine miracles followed their ministries everywhere they went. They were so yielded to the Holy Spirit that God used them to write the New Testament scriptures.

Yet, there is no record in their writings or any writings later written about them, that tells anything about blood or oil oozing from their bodies during their ministries.

The Lord Jesus Christ had *"the Spirit without measure,"* yet no oozing oil accompanied Him during His earthly ministry — and He never shed an ounce of His blood until His agony in the garden of Gethsemane and His crucifixion at Golgotha.

Besides this, her fantastic story reeked of the spiritual activity that occurs in Third World countries where paganism is rampant. In those highly superstitious countries, people are prone to believe in and even worship statues that cry and paintings of the crucifixion which they say really bleed.

Because there is no evidence for such signs and wonders recorded in God's Word — *and God's Word must be our stan-*

dard — our Biblically-based conclusion must be that if this was in fact a real supernatural phenomena, it had no precedent in scripture, and therefore, should not be taken seriously as a "sign and wonder" from God. There simply was no scriptural substantiation for it.

The Blood and Oil Sign

Unfortunately, now my suspicions and uneasy feelings had been confirmed. Evidence had come forward to prove she was, at least in part, a fraud.

I thought, "Oh, great! This is not what we needed — an imposter panning off a fake sign and wonder under the guise of the anointing."

Her last stunt, the one my friend was telling me about and the one that exposed her as a charlatan, was unquestionably one of the most ridiculous counterfeits that I had heard of in years. Her "supernatural manifestations" were getting more sensational and bizarre all the time!

First, she had her "blood sign," which I discovered after research, was not a new phenomena at all.

This strange phenomena of nail prints mysteriously appearing in the hands and feet, a pierced brow, a pierced side and a lashed back, go all the way back to the Dark Ages, to the year A.D. 1224, when these mysterious bleeding lacerations first appeared on the body of the well-known friar, St. Francis of Assisi.

Regardless of where St. Francis' "stigmata" came from (that is not the topic of this book), since those early days when he was first "stigmatized," more than 300 different individuals throughout the world have experienced this same horrible and grueling, pain-stricken condition.

There was Emile Biccheria (1238-1278) who bore *the marks of a crown of thorns;* Elizabeth of Kerkenrode (1275) who went through the *re-enactment of the crucifixion every twenty-four hours, beating her body so hard and loud, until it could be heard blocks away from her home;* Helen Brumsin (1285), a Dominican nun, *whose back was terribly mutilated with the marks of a vicious scourging;* Padre Pio (1887-1968), who found his hands bleeding after complaining of *a stinging sensation in the middle of his palms;* and Therese Neumann (1898-1962), *who had bleeding from her shoulder* — supposedly where Christ had carried the cross — *and bleeding from her knees, hands, feet, back, side, forehead and eyelids.*

During many of Therese Neumann's bleeding episodes, she claimed to have visions during which she said she could hear Jesus speaking in perfect Aramaic and later claimed to be divinely healed of paralysis (resulting from an earlier stroke), while she had a vision of the Assumption of Mary.

This short list only covers five documented cases, leaving at least another 295 documented cases that are too long, horrid and detailed to cover in this chapter.

It is interesting to note, that in nearly every one of the 300 known cases that are documented, exceedingly strange psychological behavior and bizarre habits accompanied the afflicted person.

When you look at the documented details surrounding the majority of stigmatic experiences, you quickly discover in nearly every case their manifestations of bleeding were also accompanied by weird dreams, visions and voices.

In fact, if you look *very closely* at the facts surrounding these cases, you will agree that many of the details sound like the activity of demon spirits.

Terrible sicknesses, bruises appearing and disappearing on the body, self-inflicted beating and self-imposed mutilation, a refusal to wear clothes, intense pain and profuse bleeding from the eyelids, from under the fingernails and so on, are all common denominators in the majority of stigmatic cases.

Do You Think this is the Work of the Holy Spirit?

If this really is a spiritual phenomena, and not a mental condition as some scholars and medical professionals have suggested, then the question must be asked: "From *which source* does this spiritual phenomena come?"

You may be asking, "Does Rick Renner have a personal vendetta against this woman?" Absolutely not! Why, then, am I belaboring this point? The reason is simple.

This case of deception, as you shall see in the pages to come, was so blatant and obvious that it reveals how serious our spiritual condition is at this time.

As a people, we are so extremely hungry for a new move of God, that we have wrongly abandoned reason, sound doctrine and common sense, in order to grab hold of anything that even appears to have the mark of the supernatural upon it — hoping that it may be the beginning of a new move of God.

Our zeal for the supernatural has, to a great extent, placed us in a very dangerous position. If we continue to reach out and accept every new supernatural manifestation that comes along without thinking, reasoning, questioning or testing it according to scripture, we will find ourselves in the same predicament, being deceived again and again.

Thus the reason for writing this book, and the reason I have chosen to use this example; not to pick on any one person, any one group, etc., but to awaken us to our need for *discernment* and *sound thinking* in these last days.

I desire a new outpouring of God's power as much as anyone else. However, we must not be so naive that Satan would send us imitations, thus robbing us of the real thing.

In this particular case, no one could question the genuineness of the marks or the scars that this new, questionable woman minister had on her body. The scars were real, the wounds were real, and the blood was real.

To make sure no trickery was involved, physicians had observed this bleeding on different occasions and confirmed it did not appear to be the result of trickery or a self-inflicted wound.

Since the phenomena appeared to be genuinely supernatural, most people accepted it as being from God. However, all supernatural phenomena doesn't necessarily come from God.

The question must be rightfully asked: "Would the same healing, delivering, saving God Who sent His Son to take our sin and pain away from us, now do this to someone?" "Is this really a supernatural work of God?" "Is it the manifestation of a bizarre mental condition?" "Or is it the activity of demon spirits?"

What Is Your Conclusion?

Further investigation of her story proved even further that sound doctrine had been abandoned in this particular case.

A testimony which she had given years earlier in her life was sufficient to show that her supernatural activity was not from God. Any honest Bible student could quickly ascertain that this emphatically does not agree with scripture in any way, shape or form.

Though this testimony was not written by her personally, it clearly had her approval and endorsement as being true. According to her own testimony, she clearly states how the oil was first supernaturally imparted to her.

She says:

"An angel came to me in a dream and told me that God was going to anoint me with oil, and that *I was to put this oil into containers and give it to people for their needs. . . .*"

The next day ". . .my hands began to feel wet. When I looked at them *a stream of oil began to flow from my finger-tips.* Overjoyed, I grabbed the first container that I could find and began to fill it up with the oil that was flowing from my hands. . . after about an hour had passed, *we had secured at least a gallon of this oil.*"[1]

Her Pitcher of Blood and Oil

She continues her story:

"In my bedroom, I had a pitcher containing oil which had flowed from my body. One night while I was sleeping, Jesus came to me in a dream. He told me that this oil was going *to turn into blood. . . .*" The next day "I saw Jesus walking toward me. As He came close, He told me that He was going to give me what He had promised.

"*At this time, Jesus leaned toward the pitcher, and blood began to fall from His forehead, where a crown of thorns had been deeply imbedded. And from the wounds in His feet, blood also began to spill into the pitcher. . . .*"

My husband "happened to walk in and there in my bedroom, his eyes were directed toward the pitcher as he saw for himself *blood settling from the top to the bottom of the oil . . .* Today I still have this treasured pitcher of blood and oil."[2]

Her Pierced Hands

Here is her own account of how her hands were pierced:

"I will never forget that Thursday night service . . . I remember sitting there in church that evening, listening to the music and clapping my hands.

"I started to feel *pain* in my hands as though *needles* were being driven into them. It was slight at first, but within a split second, the *pain* became almost unbearable. *I cringed as I saw blood seeping forth from my palms.*"[3]

Her Pierced Feet

"I began to see what looked like a heavy cloud forming in the bedroom. . . It frightened me as it began to thicken and form into a shape.

"I lay perfectly still as I watched it materialize before my eyes and walk toward me as it took the appearance of a white robe. . . As this form of a man reached down, he touched me with his hand, and at that same instance, I felt such *a terrible sharp pain.*

"*I immediately looked down at my feet only to see that they had been pierced...* I called out (to husband) and he came running into the room. Together, we stared at my feet as *blood began to run from the pierce marks down the sides of my feet on the bed....*"[4]

Her Pierced Brow

"After what seemed like only minutes of prayer, I felt a great and sudden fatigue on my body. My strength began to drain and I felt like a tremendous weight had been unloaded upon me. The pressure became so great that *pain began to surge my body, especially my head.* I was burdened so heavily that sweat began to pour from my head... I lay there on the floor unable to move my body.

"My mind was submerged with *pain and grief...* The *agony* increased until I could bear no more... I went into the bathroom to wash my face, and there I stood in amazement, staring into the mirror as I saw *great drops of blood running from my forehead.* There were wounds all around as though someone had pushed a crown into my head...."[5]

Her Whipped Back

"Three nights later I was standing on the platform... I had just stepped forward to begin to speak when out of nowhere *a mighty cracking sound split the air...* It was so startling that no one knew what was happening... Then, without warning and just as thunderous as the first, another crashing sound lashed out and broke the stillness....

"At this exact moment, my hands involuntarily clutched my back, when *a pain such as I have never before experienced struck viciously across my shoulders...* I could never explain the *agony* of this supernatural experience, except to say that my back was being *unmercifully striped with an unseen whip....*"[6]

Her Pierced Side

"A day or two later, I was at home praying... Just then I began to see a vision. *A dark form suddenly appeared and started coming toward me. . .* As the figure neared, it began to materialize and I could see that it was a man carrying something in his hand. At last, *to my horror,* I saw that it was *a long, shining spear. . .* I lay limp beneath the power of God and watched as *he lifted the weapon and put it to my side.*

"I could feel the sharp point being pressed against my side, then all at once, he plunged it deep into my flesh. My body trembled against the pain and coldness of the spear that was being driven into my side."

My husband "came home to find me lying on the floor with *blood seeping from my side.* He lifted my garment and there he could see the *bloody wound of the spear which had pierced my side.*"[7]

How Could This Go Unnoticed?

Taking the Word of God as our basis for truth, we must ask: "Is this the work of the Holy Spirit?"

What are your conclusions? Does this sound like the work of the Holy Spirit to you?

This sounds more like a demonic attack and vicious beating, doesn't it? Even more, it lines up and falls into perfect agreement with the other 300 documented cases that are known.

Yet, these lacerations and brandmarks were heralded as the evidence of a divine visitation of God upon a young "handmaiden" who was available.

Where has our common sense gone?

How could anyone who knows God really believe that He would unmercifully beat someone across the back with a vicious scourging? Why would God want to turn a pitcher of oil into blood? *What is the purpose of this?*

Would the same God who sent Jesus into the world, really raise a long, shining spear and thrust it into the side of a young woman, thus causing her to bleed profusely? Does this sound like God? Of course not!

9

Still, with all of these facts available, she began to gain widespread acceptance in our Charismatic ranks. How in the world could this go unnoticed?

Chapter Two
A Blatant Case of Deception

Her deceptive activities reminded me of another case of deception that occurred during the 1970's, when another charlatan told a story so dramatic that she traveled all across the nation, drawing mammoth crowds of thrilled listeners as she sold them a lie.

What a story she had to tell! Earlier in life, according to her story, physicians had removed both of her breasts in a radical mastectomy because of a spreading cancer.

This cancer, as she reported in her testimony, was so severe that it had spread into her brain and nearly every organ of the body you could think to name. She related how she had visited several leading cancer clinics, who tried experimental drugs on her and used her as a medical guinea pig because they knew she would never recover.

After bringing captivated audiences to tears over her terrible, hopeless condition, then the story of her "miracle" would begin. It was a *sensational* story; just the kind of marvelous, miraculous testimony that we love to hear.

I can remember taking a cassette tape of her testimony in hand and slipping it into my tape recorder. As I listened, what I heard was so deeply moving that I could not hold back my tears. I sobbed as I heard how God had done a creative miracle in this poor woman's body. I was so touched by her tender testimony, that I made copies of the tape and handed it out to those we knew who were dying of terminal cancer.

Her story was *phenomenal.* While people sat in their seats, listening, breathing sighs of relief and giving thanks to God for her fantastic miracle, she told crowds how God restored both of her breasts one night while she was sleeping.

According to her story, she went to bed one night a cancer-stricken, terminally ill patient with the horrible scars of a radical mastectomy.

But the next morning, when she was awakened, to her amazement both breasts had been *completely restored.* And even more — this miracle, she declared, was so complete that there weren't even any scars left on her body from the harsh surgery that had been performed on her.

This was back when the Charismatic Movement was in full swing. Most of us during those days were fresh out of denominational churches, just recently filled with the Holy Spirit, and were hungry to hear about God's power to heal. Miracles such as the one just related to you were not uncommon at that time. God was truly pouring out His Spirit and miracles abounded.

The problem wasn't her fantastic claim of healing. Of course God could do this. Then what was the problem? *This woman never had cancer.*

Her story was *completely fabricated.* In time, as always is the case with frauds, false prophets and false teachers, her story became *terribly exaggerated.*

Finally, toward the end of her ravaging of the saints, she became so immersed in her own deception, that she began removing her blouse and undergarments to reveal how perfectly God had restored her breasts. Behind closed doors, before her meetings began, she would take key women leaders aside *to privately show what marvelous things God had done.*

I remember the frustration key spiritual leaders experienced when they discovered the truth and attempted to alert others to her deception. Rather than rejoice that God had protected them from this imposter, these protective spiritual leaders were accused of a "lack of faith" for not believing her story, and were accused of "going on a witch-hunt."

That was years ago.

New Manifestations of the Holy Spirit?

Now, as my friend told me about this new event with the blood and oil woman and her supernatural "feathers," I heard something which sounded just as outrageous as the story just related to you. This "feather" incident was a blatant attempt to "merchandise" something sensational in order to make a gain of the saints.

This self-proclaimed prophetess walked back and forth on the platform before the huge crowd that evening. She told the great mass of people to "shut their eyes and worship Jesus."

While their eyes were shut and they were truly worshipping the Lord, she began dropping white feathers all across the stage. Then, suddenly, as though she was shocked at what she had found, she told everyone to open their eyes and to look, *to behold something supernatural!*

She told the people that the Holy Spirit had flown over the crowd like a dove while they were worshipping the Lord. She exclaimed that He had even left a remnant of His presence. . . .

Here it came! She was getting ready to produce a new act — pure sensationalism for the sake of attracting and holding crowds. She had been regularly manifesting blood and oil in her meetings around the area for some time and this was getting to be an old phenomena.

In order to keep the saints mesmerized with her special powers, it is evident she felt that she needed something new, something exciting, and something that no one else was doing! *Here it came. . . .*

The false prophetess began walking around the platform in the large auditorium, pointing here and there toward all the places where she had dropped her white feathers. *Only she espoused that these were the Holy Spirit's feathers!*

As the story was related to me, I thought, "That's strange, I didn't know the Holy Spirit was a bird. Where is *that* in the Word of God?"

The Bible does teach that John the Baptist saw "the Spirit of God descending like a dove, and lighting upon Jesus" (Matthew 3:16). However, it does not say he saw *a dove;* but he saw the Spirit descending *"like a dove."*

This in no way teaches that the Holy Spirit is a dove or a bird. Rather, John the Baptist saw the Spirit light upon Jesus like a dove, *or with the gentleness of a dove.* This is symbolic language to let us know about the gentle nature of the Holy Spirit. He is *like a dove; not a dove.*

Is This the Dark Ages?

It sounded a little bit like something right out of the Dark Ages to me. A crash course on the Middle Ages would make it plain to any reader that this was nothing more than a repeat from the past.

During the Dark Ages, people claimed to possess *genuine splinters of the cross that Jesus died on at Golgotha;* that was when some claimed to own some of *the real blood of Jesus and kept it in little bottles as a relic of the Lord;* some said they owned *straw from Jesus' original manger; pieces of His garments;* and yes, believe it or not, during the Dark Ages, *some even claimed to possess "feathers" that were accidently dropped by the Holy Spirit.* These were called "relics of the Holy Spirit."

These kinds of tricks are always easy to pander on people who are unfounded in God's Word. As Hosea 4:6 says, "My people are destroyed for lack of knowledge." It is easy to pull tricks off on people who are not educated in God's Word. They have no sense of discernment.

This feather trick was nothing new. It was a piece of the Dark Ages rehashed, repackaged and being sold to a brand new group. I was appalled that anyone would try to pass this off as a genuine "miracle" in front of modern-day believers who were supposed to be strong in the Word.

But there was something more appalling than this! The people seemed to believe that it was a real manifestation of the Holy Spirit! It made me wonder if these people were really as established in the Word of God as they thought. If they knew the Word so well, where was their sense of discernment?

I thought to myself, *"Sure, Holy Spirit 'feathers!' Someone pinch me and tell me if this is the 20th Century or the 1200's of the Dark Ages?"* I jokingly asked, *"Is this the new move of God?" "Are we now headed for a Feather Movement?"*

Documented Deception

I had to see this with my own eyes. I located someone with a video of the event and could hardly believe my eyes as I viewed the video on the screen in front of me that day. I said, *"Wait, wait, wait. . . would you please rewind that tape so I could see that part one more time?"*

I leaned forward toward the television screen to look as closely as I could. And to my amazement, there it was, just as I had heard — a fake sign and wonder — a feather trick — and it was being done in front of hundreds of sincere, spiritually hungry believers.

The video was put on slow motion to make sure every movement of the hand could be seen as feathers were dropped by this "prophetess" around the stage.

It appeared that she was manipulating the feathers out of her handkerchief. This exhibition was no more than a magician's sleight of hand. At one point, you could actually see her passing feathers from one hand to the other as she prepared to drop them on the floor. There was no doubt that this was a fraud. *It was documented.*

Let me say something very important at this point for

the sake of the other ministers who were present that week at this large Christian gathering, and for the sake of those who hosted the event. I do not intend to suggest that any of the other ministers who were present, agreed or approved of what this self-proclaimed prophetess did that evening.

Many of these other ministries were not even aware that this woman was going to be there that night and would not have come had they known she was going to be a part of the agenda. Some later told me they were already wise to her ways and had specifically asked if she was going to be there. Upon discovering she was a participant, they refused to be a part lest they should become associated with her.

Some good ministry took place in other services that week. Unfortunately, this feather trick hung over the entire event like a horrible, nasty shadow. This is especially sad when you consider the wonderful ministries who traveled great distances and took time to minister that week and to be publicly classified with this fraud.

Deceived by a Professional Deceiver

As I watched the video, a horrible inward sorrow came into my spirit as I beheld hundreds of sincere, spiritually hungry believers begin praising God for this "new" sign and wonder.

Then there was the other group of people — the group who got up and filed out the back doors of the auditorium. They were confused and asked questions such as: "Where in the Word of God does it mention a 'feather manifestation?'" "Is there any scriptural basis for this?"

Yet, none of the other well-known spiritual leaders who were present stood up to oppose what had happened or publicly questioned what had just occurred. *They were silent.*

An Uneasy Situation

Like many other people who have asked since this event

16

took place, I also asked: *"Why didn't the crowd recognize this was a fake?"* *"Where was their sense of discernment?"* *"What about the big-name leaders that were present?"* Some of these are well-known ministers. Why did they believe this lie — *or did they?*

I tend to believe most of the leaders present didn't believe the lie that was passed off that night. They were simply so *shocked* they didn't know what to do.

Like everyone else, their eyes had been shut and they had been worshipping the Lord while this fraud dropped the feathers around the stage. When they opened their eyes, they were just as surprised as everyone else. *Besides, would anyone dare to do such a blatant, dastardly deed in front of so many people?*

The answer is clearly "yes." It was obvious that a false prophetess was in the camp and this prophetess was attempting to "merchandise" something exciting and sensational to the saints once again.

A Neutral Mind is not a Sign of Spirituality

Contrary to what some have implied in recent days, shifting your mind into neutral is not a sign of spirituality.

Some prophets and teachers today imply that rational thinking is unspiritual and carnal. The idea is suggested that if you examine or scrutinize a new doctrine, a new teaching, a radical statement, someone's visit with Jesus or an angel, or some other type of new supernatural occurrence, then you are in rebellion, unbelief and sin.

Letting your mind slip into a state of neutrality is not a sign of spirituality; it may be a sign of stupidity. *God gave you your mind!* The Holy Spirit doesn't come to remove your mind, rather, He comes to illuminate your mind! True spiritual people should have quick, intelligent, sharp minds! Illumination and enlightenment is what the Holy Spirit brings us.

However, as the crowds rose up from their seats to see

the feathers that night, the false prophetess quoted from First Corinthians 2:14 and told the crowd if they questioned what they saw, it was because "the natural man receiveth not the things of the Spirit of God."

The implication seems to be: "take your brain out, put it on a shelf, believe anything we tell you to believe and question absolutely nothing." The thought continues, "If you question something done in the name of the anointing, you're in the flesh. Your natural man is trying to talk you out of the supernatural."

A Real Miracle Will Always Pass the Test

However, if a supernatural manifestation is really from God, it can be scrutinized, examined, tested and will still be affirmed as a genuine miracle. You *can't* hurt a miracle by examining it. A real miracle will be verified by investigation.

But a counterfeit or trick will never stand up to such a test. Because of this, you can be sure a counterfeit prophet or teacher will always tell you not to think, reason or question anything you see. They know if you dig very deep, the "wonder" will fall apart.

We must not abandon reason and sound doctrine for the sake of spiritual hunger and a new move of God.

Just because a supernatural manifestation occurs inside the walls of a church or at a Christian gathering, does not mean it is a valid miracle or a manifestation of the power of God. This false prophetess is a perfect example of a false manifestation being performed right in a church gathering. *It is not wrong to think, ask questions or to seek the truth.*

A Warning for Those Who Imitate the Anointing

Of course we want to see miracles! Of course we desire a new move of the Holy Spirit's power! However, we must learn to recognize *the difference* between the real and the false, so Satan cannot pander fake manifestations in our midst, thus aborting the genuine move of the Spirit which God desires to pour forth in these days.

The anointing of God is so precious that God will not permit His precious anointing to be imitated. In fact, God issues *a strong warning* to those who would try to imitate the anointing oil in Exodus 30:33. The verse reads, "Whosoever compoundeth any like it (i.e., "whosoever imitates it") or whosoever putteth any of it upon a stranger, shall even be cut off from his people."

Then, to make sure the warning is heard loud and clear, God repeats the warning again five verses later. "Whosoever shall make like unto that, to smell thereto, shall even be cut off from his people" (verse 38).

As we proceed in this book, you will see the Bible speaks plainly to us regarding these issues and regarding those who come to "merchandise the anointing." But first, we must ask another very important question:

Should We Sweep False Prophets Under the Carpet and Pretend the Problem Doesn't Exist?

After this feather incident occurred, controversy, arguments and intense disagreements erupted across the nation between several ministries.

Why did disagreements and harsh feelings develop between some ministries after this event was exposed as a fraud? *There are several reasons.*

First, and understandably so, some leaders who had previously believed in this woman's ministry and had even promoted her, felt "put on the spot."

They were concerned that this ridiculous situation would make them appear to have no spiritual discernment at all. To make matters worse, some of them were her associates prior to this. While they were well-qualified and anointed ministers themselves, they feared people would wonder if they were involved in the same kind of charlatan activities.

I am quite certain they didn't want to be lumped together with her just because they had been affiliated with her in past meetings and conferences. I can understand why they felt this way. I would probably have felt that way too.

An Attempt to "Save Face?"

This ugly mess cast a shadow on how well they had heard the voice of God. If they were really spiritually in-tune, why didn't they perceive she was a fraud?

This act of deception was so blatant it made one wonder if they were able to recognize the real anointing of God at all. Therefore, the prophetic camp was fearful that people would rightfully ask, *"Couldn't these other prophets hear God's voice any better than that?"*

Some of these ministers are powerful men and women of God and are definitely marked with a tremendous anointing and are accompanied with genuine signs and wonders. Yet, they were "taken" by this "counterfeit." Therefore, some of them would have preferred that the issue be dealt with privately, rather than publicly.

Was this an attempt to "save face" as some have suggested?

Is this a "Witch-Hunt?"

Then there was the other group who felt this issue was too hot and serious to be dealt with privately. This group was primarily made up of Bible teachers. "Since she did this publicly," they said, "she should be exposed publicly." It was easy for me to see this point of view too.

The real issue at hand wasn't whether or not this fraud should be dealt with or exposed, but *how* it should be done. The two groups began to form and leaders seemed to be taking sides. Though not true entirely, to the natural eye it looked like a dreadful match of *teachers against prophets, and prophets against teachers.*

It wasn't long until division, disagreement and discord developed. Those of the prophetic camp, who had been associated with this false prophetess in the past, accused the other group, the teachers, of "going on a witch-hunt."

In response to this, the teacher camp, who wanted to deal with the issue publicly, accused the other side of "sweeping the issue under the carpet for the sake of protecting their pride."

Questions We Must Answer Today

Thus the issue has been raised: *"How do you deal with a false prophet or false teacher?"*

How do you recognize the characteristics of a false prophet or false teacher? If you come across one, do you simply shut your eyes and hope the situation will change? Do you pretend that you never saw something wrong happen? Do you deny that hesitation in your spirit and hope for the best? Do you sweep it under the carpet and pretend the event never occurred?

What if a genuine prophet or teacher begins to take on the characteristics of a false prophet or false teacher? Do you deal with it privately, so as to protect those who are in the ministry and have been previously associated with this person?

Do you tell the Body of Christ at large when a false prophet or false teacher is in the camp, so they can develop a sense of discernment regarding these kinds of things? Do you ignore the fact that these things happen and leave the people open to further counterfeits and shams?

What if a prophet or teacher refuses to submit to a local pastor? Should they be required to be a member of a local church? What are leaders supposed to do when such situations present themselves?

Are there answers for these questions?

Let the Bible be our Guide

When personal emotions regarding such issues are raging so strong, we cannot depend upon our own sense of judgment. Therefore, we must turn to the Bible and let the Bible be our guide.

Therefore, the real question is: *"What does the Bible say?" "What is the New Testament, Biblical precedent for dealing with false prophets, false teachers and heretics?"*

Don't Throw the Baby Out

It has been said, "Don't throw the baby out with the bathwater!" Likewise, we must *not* throw out all supernatural phenomena because of a few bad experiences with counterfeits and frauds.

I was recently visiting with a solid, respectable prophet who said to me, "You know, Rick, rather than be associated with all the silliness that's going on right now in the Body of Christ, I'd rather just back away from my gift." He continued, "Today if you're a prophet, people immediately put you in some weird, crazy prophet category."

I responded, "You're the kind of prophet that we need in the Body of Christ! Please don't abandon us to all the flakes out there. We need solid, well-grounded prophetic ministry!"

If good prophets and teachers step out of their places at this critical time in the history of the Church, it will leave an open door for all the false ministries to emerge into a place of prominence. *God forbid!*

This strange phenomena of false prophets and false teachers moving into prominent positions is exactly what the apostles had to confront in the early days of the Church. In First Timothy 4:1, the Holy Spirit prophesied that the Church in the "latter times" would have to confront it too.

Chapter Three
A Breeding Ground for Spiritual Excess

Before we go any further into this book, *let me say that all prophets and teachers are not false.* Thank God, there are wonderful, genuine prophets and teachers in the Church of Jesus Christ today and we desperately need their sound ministries!

By writing this book and dealing with this serious subject, I do *not* intend to suggest that all prophets and teachers are off-base. This is not the case at all!

According to Ephesians 4:11, Jesus Christ gave these gifts to the Church for the "maturing of the saints." We need the ministry of well-grounded prophets and teachers, perhaps now, more than ever before.

Thus, the reason that the attack of false prophets and false teachers is so serious and critical in our day. By sending false ministry gifts into our midst, Satan's plan is to burn people so badly with spiritual excess, that they will reject the genuine manifestation of the Spirit altogether.

Therefore, we must develop a sense of discernment about these things and know what the Bible teaches about *false ministries,* as well as true ministries. There have always been "wolves in sheep's clothing" and according to the scripture, this problem isn't going to go away any time soon.

Drawing a Line of Division and Separation

My dictionary says true "division" is: 1) the act or process of dividing; an instance of being divided in opinion; disagreement and disunity *to avoid being exploited,* especially between two groups; something that *divides, separates or marks off;* the act of *separating* or *keeping apart."*

After studying the chapters to come, it is my prayer that God's Word will be taught so clearly and explicitly that you will have God-imparted discernment to know the difference between true and false ministries — *so that you will be able to keep them separated from one another.*

On this false prophet and false teacher issue, the Word of God draws a straight line. False prophets and false teachers are placed on one side of that line, and the real gifts are placed on the other side of that line.

By defining their behavior and characteristics so explicitly in scripture, the Word of God serves as a protector for us and for the real prophets and teachers who are hurt by this invasion of falsehood perhaps more than anyone else.

If we would heed what the Word has to say on this subject, we would be able to keep these two divided from each other; marked off; separated from each other; and therefore, God's people would cease to be *spiritually exploited.*

Our Worst Reaction

Our worst reaction would be to reject all ministry altogether. This is Satan's very plan! Therefore, we must take Paul's command to "quench not the Spirit" very seriously.

In First Thessalonians 5:19-20, Paul commanded us, "Quench not the Spirit. Despise not prophesyings. Prove all things; hold fast that which is good."

Quenching the Spirit and despising prophesyings is not the proper response to this problem. If anything at all, false prophets and false teachers confirm that there are real prophets and teachers which we need.

Any of the fivefold ministry gifts can be counterfeited. In Second Corinthians 11:13, Paul plainly tells us that there are "false apostles." In Second Peter 2:1, Peter alerts us to the reality of "false teachers"; in Matthew 7:15, Jesus tells us to beware of "false prophets"; and in John 10:12, the Lord speaks of "hirelings" or "false pastors."

By dealing with the issue of false prophets and false teachers in this book, I do not suggest that only *these* can be imitated by Satan. Anything good that God does, Satan attempts to invade, distort, twist and pervert. This is his nature.

However, there was a false prophet and false teacher problem during the days of the apostles, and according to First Timothy 4:1, there will be a tremendous problem with the ministries of sensational and mystifying men once again in the latter times.

The purpose of this book is to see what the Word has to say about false ministry. Thank God for the true, but we must also know the marks of the false.

With a greater sense of discernment in operation, we will be able to easily recognize the difference between the false and the true, and thus protect the Body of Christ and the ministry of well-grounded, tested and proven prophets and teachers.

For those who flow in questionable ministry, this book will not be their friend. Neither were the apostles. They spoke hard and strong about things that did not line up with apostolic teaching and scripture. Neither did they flinch when they described the marks of a false prophet and false teacher.

For those who are tested, balanced and well-grounded, this book will be a source of encouragement. My prayer is that this book will help to build a broader base for their acceptance. We must thank God and pray for these God-sent ministries who have a genuine word from heaven for the Church in this late hour of history.

Living in the Latter Times

However, before we begin our intensive study of the scriptures that deal with the characteristics or marks of false ministry, we must first turn to First Timothy 4:1, to see what the Holy Spirit declared through Paul about this spiritual attack on the Church in the last days.

Because this verse is such a powerful statement from the Spirit and is foundational to what we will see later in this book, we will dissect it and study it thoroughly in this chapter to see what type of spiritual environment, especially in the last days, will produce a breeding ground for false prophets and false teachers.

In First Timothy 4:1, Paul said, "Now the Spirit speaketh expressly, that in the latter times some shall depart from the faith, giving heed to seducing spirits and doctrines of demons."

Pay careful attention to the phrase "speaketh expressly." This important phrase is from the Greek word *rhetos* (rhe-tos), and is one of the most familiar words in the New Testament. It is from the same Greek root that we derive the well-known and often-used word, *rhema*.

It describes something that is "spoken clearly, umistakably, vividly, undeniably," or something that is "unquestionable, certain and definite."

By selecting to use this word, the Holy Spirit is making His point absolutely "clear." The future events which He is about to describe through Paul are *definite*; they will *certainly* come to pass; therefore, he speaks in *undeniable terms.*

You could actually translate the verse, "Now the Spirit speaks in *absolutely clear words. . . .*" "Now the Spirit speaks in *unmistakable terms. . . .*" "Now the Spirit speaks in *undeniable, definite words. . . .*" Or, you could even translate it, "Now the Spirit speaks in the *strongest and clearest of language. . . .*"

Then Paul continues to give us this undeniable and unmistakable message. He says, "Now the Spirit speaketh expressly that in the latter times, some shall depart from the faith. . . ."

A Prophetic Warning for the Church

This phrase "latter times" is important too. The Holy Spirit is now, through this verse, alerting a last day's generation to a dangerous plot which Satan will conspire to use against the Church.

Though there have been many spiritual attacks on the Church through two millenniums, this attack in the "latter times" will be especially severe. Thus the reason that the Holy Spirit uses such strong language. In fact, this last day's assault on the Church is considered so serious by the Spirit, that He now speaks to us in *"absolutely clear, unmistakable, vivid, undeniable, certain and definite words."*

Notice that Paul even tells us when this attack will occur. He specifically states it will take place in the "latter times."

The word "latter" comes from the Greek word *husteros* (hu-ste-ros) and is normally used for emphasizing the very *extreme end* of something. On the other hand, the word "times" comes from the Greek word *kairos* (kai-ros) which always describes a "season" or a "special, allotted, designated period of time."

When taken together as one complete phrase, the words "latter times" describe "the very last season" or "the very last period of time." Keeping it in context, it describes the "latter times" of the Church age and the activities that are characteristic of that "last season."

These are the Greek words we would use to describe the very last day of the year, the very last day of the month, or even the very last day of the week. They denote the *ultimate end of a thing*.

Therefore, in A.D. 63, the approximate time when First

Timothy was written, the Holy Spirit pointed His prophetic finger toward the future nearly 2,000 years and prophesied what would occur in the Church in the "very last times." What He saw then was so alarming that He alerted us to it with the "strongest and clearest of words."

The Spirit's message is unmistakable! What did He see prophetically that was so alarming to Him about our current generation?

A Departure from the Faith

The verse continues to say, "Now the Spirit speaketh expressly, that in the latter times *some shall depart from the faith. . . .*"

The Holy Spirit was alarmed because He could foresee a day when people would begin to "depart from the faith."

The word "depart" is especially important because it tells us more than simply the idea of "departing." This word actually details the slow methods and seducing process by which the enemy will create this departure.

"Depart" is from the Greek word *aphistemi* (a-phi-ste-mi), which is a compound of two Greek words. The first word means "away," and the second word means "to stand."

When compounded together, this word means "to stand or to step away from," "to withdraw from," or "to shrink back away from." It is from this same Greek word that we derive the word "apostate."

How does "apostasy" take place in a believer's life? How does a committed believer become so seduced that eventually he or she begins "to withdraw, shrink back away from" and eventually "depart from the faith?"

This Greek word for "departing" explicitly tells us this type of departure takes place *very slowly.* In fact, it occurs so slowly that most who are "departing from the faith" will not even realize that this departure is taking place.

28

This means "departing from the faith" *doesn't* refer to a blatant, outright rejection of the faith. It is much more *subtle* than that. This refers to a careful, slow, almost unnoticeable, inch-by-inch, step-by-step departing from the faith over a period of time. This is a very slow "shrinking back and withdrawal."

Please notice that the Word *doesn't* say they will *reject* the faith, it says they will *depart* from the faith. There is a great difference between rejecting the faith and departing from the faith. *Rejecting is deliberate; departing is slow and unintentional.*

Sincere, but Sincerely Wrong

This verse outlines how the devil, has in the past, does in the present, and will in the future, attempt to seduce spiritually hungry, sincere believers. He takes advantage of their desire for more of God and His power, and skillfully seduces them into imbalance in the guise of a deeper spirituality.

Let me explain. Every sincere, spiritually hungry believer has two innate, God-given needs in his or her life. They are resident in all believers regardless of background or locality. The first of these two innate needs is spiritual sustenance to feed the inner man: *the Word.*

This required spiritual meat fulfills our deep need for more understanding of God. Over the passage of time, this type of consistent teaching produces spiritual growth. It is *impossible* to attain spiritual maturity without feeding on sound doctrine. This is a *required diet* for everyone who desires to grow in God.

This first deep, basic need for the Word should not be viewed as an elementary beginning for younger believers only. Feeding on God's Word is for all believers, regardless of how long they have walked with the Lord, how much they have already heard, or how much knowledge they already possess. Every believer *must* feed on God's Word in order to grow.

Peter told the young, new believer, "As new born babes, desire the sincere milk of the word, that ye may grow thereby" (First Peter 2:2). This "milk of the word" nourishes the young believer's innate desire for more knowledge of God.

For the older and more mature believer, Hebrews 5:14 says, "But strong meat belongeth to them that are of full age, even to those who by reason of use have their senses exercised to discern both good and evil."

According to this verse, even those Christians who are of "full age" need the Word to fulfill their ongoing, God-given desire for more knowledge of God. This is our first, innate, God-given need.

The second need of every sincere, spiritually hungry believer is for spiritual experience. Knowledge alone never satisfies the inner cravings of man for God. Man also craves to know His supernatural power.

In First Corinthians 8:1, Paul plainly states that knowledge just for the sake of knowledge, eventually causes a person to be "puffed up."

Knowledge just for knowledge's sake will never fulfill the needs of our inner man by itself. In addition to knowledge, we must have a constant flow of God's power in our lives to satisfy our deep inner need for the supernatural.

Paul recognized man's need for both the Word and power. Thus, he said, "For our gospel came not unto you in word only, but also in power, and in the Holy Ghost, and in much assurance" (First Thessalonians 1:5).

The Lord Himself recognized this inner need of man. For this reason, He "worked with them, confirming the Word with signs following" (Mark 16:20). And Hebrews 2:4 adds further support to our need for this *divine mixture* of the Word and God's power. It says, "God also bearing them witness, both with signs and wonders, and with divers miracles, and gifts of the Holy Ghost, according to His own will."

If we pit one of these against the other, though sincere,

we are sincerely wrong. It is not either/or, but rather *both*. We must feed on the teaching of God's Word, and pursue His power at the same time.

From One Ditch to the Next Ditch

The devil knows that you have these passionate desires for the Word and the supernatural. He knows that *both* of these are *essential* in order for you to be fulfilled spiritually and for you to become a powerful, Spirit-filled believer.

Therefore, he attempts to throw you off into the ditch in one of these areas. On one side of the road, there is the ditch of Christianity with no power. On the other side of the road, is a ditch where there is great zeal and hunger for God, but little teaching of God's Word and Biblical foundation. These are primarily the two types of imbalance which he conspires to throw the Church into.

The first imbalance is the preaching of the Word with no power, no signs and wonders and no supernatural manifestations.

Chrisitianity without the supernatural is the equivalent of a lifeless and dead Christianity. The Church was born in the power of the Spirit and must still, today, be maintained in the power of the Spirit.

Without the constant supernatural activity of the Holy Spirit in the Church, we are nothing more than a human benefit society. This is precisely the imbalance which the devil has thrown at the majority of the denominational world. *It is orthodoxy with no power; a lifeless and dead Christianity.*

The second imbalance has to do with an abnormal preoccupation with the sensational and spectacular.

While we must pursue God's supernatural power in our lives, it is wrong to allow signs and wonders to usurp the centrality of God's Word. When this occurs, and signs and wonders become our primary goal — the focal point of all our attention — it always results in spiritual excess of the worst kind.

This type of Christianity is normally characterized by people who have little stability in their spiritual lives, are lacking in personal holiness, and eventually, this can result in a shallow, superficial, "please give me a goose bump feeling" Christianity.

In time, the power that was genuinely present at one time disappears since there is no Word being preached for the Holy Spirit to confirm — and nothing more than sensational tales and stories are left behind.

This type of Christianity, if held to and maintained for long periods of time, will produce spiritual rot in the Church. *Neither is this an example of a healthy Christianity.*

Most Christians live their spiritual lives going from one ditch to the other. Finally! They begin to become established in the Word — and for some reason, they forget to seek God's power. Or finally! A believer gets plugged into the Spirit's power — and then forgets that he or she still needs the Word.

Rather than go from one ditch to the next, and accuse the people in the other side of the ditch of being "off," we must learn to walk "circumspectly."

In Ephesians 5:15, Paul commanded us, "See then that ye walk circumspectly, not as fools, but as wise." The word "circumspectly" is from the Greek word *akribos* (a-kri-bos) and means "to walk carefully, accurately" or "to walk right down the middle of the road."

This was not supposed to be a tug-of-war between one or the other — the Word or the supernatural. *Rather, we must learn to function in both of them simultaneously.*

In order to "walk carefully, accurately" or "right down the middle of the road of balance," we must maintain *a fierce desire for as much teaching of God's Word as we can get, and must continually stir ourselves up with a passionate desire to move in God's power.*

Taking Advantage of a Vacuum

However, according to First Timothy 4:1, in the "latter

times" the devil will try to seduce some believers away from the Word into an abnormal preoccupation with signs and wonders, new revelations, supernatural phenomena and into the sensational and the spectacular.

As a matter of fact, the Bible doesn't say that the devil will simply *try* to do this. The Bible explicitly states the devil will definitely *achieve* this in the lives of "some." The Word says, ". . . some shall depart from the faith, giving heed to seducing spirits and doctrines of demons."

Why they are "departing from the faith" is not stated. However, the reason is *implied*. The phrase "giving heed to seducing spirits and doctrines of demons" indicates they are looking for some type of deeper revelation, or something that is more spectacular than what they already have.

Perhaps they are "departing from the faith" because of disappointment. Perhaps they are disappointed, tired and saddened that the Word of God and teaching of scripture hasn't produced a supernatural revival as quickly as they desired.

Perhaps, because of this delay, they are beginning to rationalize that a God-sent revival isn't going to come through the methods they've been using. So they begin to open their minds to *other possibilities* and *other avenues* for experience. Out of a sincere desire for more of God, they turn their ears toward other, yet untried ways of getting God to move.

This is an especially dangerous possibility when there is a great vacuum of God's power in the Church. Even when faithful people hear the Word week after week, hear about healing, how to stand on the Word, how to believe God, etc., but see only a small measure of supernatural power manifested in their personal lives, they become *disillusioned*.

In this atmosphere of believing and waiting, the mind begins to wonder, "Am I on the right track?" The idea is suggested, "Maybe you should leave this and try something else."

If you have not already decided to walk "circumspect-ly" between the Word and the power, you will be tempted to abandon the Word, leave your old methods behind and teaching aside, *and turn to something else that looks more inviting and exciting.* It may even appear to be something that could spice up your spiritual life and give you a spiritual shot in the arm!

No one who genuinely loves the Lord wakes up one day and out-of-the-clear-blue says, "Gee, I think I've heard all of the Word of God that I need. What I need now is a new supernatural manifestation and a brand new, never-before-known revelation. We've had enough of the Word. Now let's go out into the realm of the Spirit."

This kind of thinking is normally a reaction to disappointment. The mind begins to think, "You've got to forget what you've been doing and try something new and exciting. Be innovative and on the 'cutting edge' of the next move of God."

They may even purport to be riding a new wave of the Spirit. We must honestly ask ourselves, "Is this really a new wave of the Spirit, or is this simply another new wind of doctrine blowing through the Church?"

While they think they are pursuing a deeper relationship with the Lord and more of the supernatural, in reality, they are stepping away from "the faith" that contains the answers they desperately need. This transition occurs *so slowly*, and is so *well disguised* by seducing spirits, that they may not even be aware that they are in transition.

Yet, a transition is taking place. These are people who once stood firmly by faith on the promises of God's Word, but now are trying some other quick-fix spiritual remedy for their problems.

Their stand is changing; their beliefs are changing; their methods are changing; their thoughts are changing; their philosophy of ministry is being altered; everything they had held to in the past is slowly being thrown out the window and new, exciting, quick-fix spiritual remedies are taking their place.

While they claim to be in pursuit of a greater spirituality, notice what it is that they are stepping away from: "some shall depart from *the faith. . . .*"

The phrase "the faith" has a definite article and is used in the objective sense, which tells us that this is not talking about raw faith, such as faith for miracles or faith for signs and wonders. Because it has a definite article and is used in the objective sense, "the faith" refers to the sound teaching of God's Word.

Therefore, a better translation of this verse could be, "some shall very slowly depart from the clear, sound teaching of the faith" — the Word!

Why Would Anyone Depart from the Faith?

Boredom has a lot to do with the reason people depart from the faith. In fact, boredom with the Word is the open door to deception. This is an especially dangerous possibility where there is a great deal of the Word of God available on a regular basis.

Individuals or cities who rarely have good teaching in their midst never become bored with the Word. Quite the contrary! When an anointed teacher comes through their town, they all show up at the meeting with pads and pencils in hand in order to take notes.

This is such a rare opportunity for them that they sit on the edge of their seats and devour each word like a starving person who is so grateful for nourishment, that he refuses to let one morsel of food fall to the ground.

But a city or a local church which has a powerful, on-going Christian influence and abundant Bible teaching, is in great danger of spiritual error. Why is this so?

The Word is so *available* in places like this, that it is possible to take the Word for granted and to become spiritually sluggish.

Those morsels of food that mean so much to the spiritually starving man, lose their importance and go unnoticed when you know another fabulous meal will be set on the table in a couple of hours. Therefore, it is easy for believers in an environment like this to develop a "take it or leave it" mentality.

A Dangerous Spiritual Predicament

Remember, it was the blessed Laodicean church who was able to say, "I am rich, and increased with goods. . . ." (Revelation 3:17).

Because they were so blessed, they lost sight of their deep, inner spiritual need. Over a period of time, they actually begin to believe that they "had need of nothing." Naturally speaking, it did appear that "they had it all."

Yet, it was to this very church that Jesus said, "Because thou art lukewarm, and neither cold nor hot, I will spue thee out of my mouth" (Revelation 3:16).

When you know the teaching of the Word, wonderful ministries, miracles, and healing meetings are available somewhere in town any ol' day of the week, it becomes a constant battle to stay excited and fresh about the move of God. *The temptation is to think that you've already seen it all, heard it all and now know it all.*

It's like a person who eats steak for every meal of the week. At first, because steak was a rarity, this was a very special treat. However, if you have steak every day, it won't be too long until you lose your *appreciation* for steak. It will become *commonplace.* Soon you'll become bored with it, even though you know you're blessed to have it.

Likewise, it is very easy to fall into a mode of ungratefulness and lack of appreciation for the things of God when you know that you can have them any ol' day of the week. In cities or churches like this, perhaps the greatest adversary is *boredom.*

This is a real battle for people who are members of a growing church that has many special speakers, teachers, visiting prophets, evangelists with healing ministries, or a church that offers its congregation a multitude of new and exciting ministries.

Those blessed of God in this way must not allow themselves to fall into the dreadful condition of lukewarmness.

The Danger of Complacency

In an environment like this, it is easy to fall into the trap of *spiritual complacency.* If you are not careful, you too will begin to think that you've seen it all and heard it all, and eventually, you can begin to even think that you know it all.

This kind of exposure for a period of time can begin to work away at your spiritual sensitivity in a profoundly negative way. Honestly, it may be harder to stay "on fire" for the Lord in an environment like this, than anywhere else in the world. Because people have seen so much, heard so much and know so much, it can all eventually become *commonplace* and *unappreciated.*

Well-known speakers in time can cease to impress you, special meetings can loose their thrill and a "big-deal" way of thinking can slowly work its way into the mainstream of the Church.

To get the attention of people who are bored like this, it is going to require something "extra special."

Even "regular miracles" can cease to hold the attention of a crowd in time. And when this situation develops, people get bored with the status quo and begin looking to spice up their spiritual life with "something new." This is the very reason the "feather" incident covered in Chapters 1 and 2 occurred. The environment was right for the introduction of something new and exciting.

A National Problem for Spirit-Filled People

This problem of complacency is now a national problem

for Spirit-filled people.

With the recent advances made in technology, the Word of God is readily available to anyone who wants it — as much of it as you want! You can even purchase a computer program that contains the Bible, Greek and Hebrew study helps, and even special Bibles to help you scan the Word more quickly to save time.

Christian publishing houses, scores of magazines and periodicals, video tapes, cassette teaching tapes, Christian television programs, radio shows and even Christian television networks have covered the land from sea-to-shining-sea.

There is no doubt about it. We are the most instructed generation of Spirit-filled people who have lived since the day of Pentecost. We truly have seen a lot, heard a lot and know a lot.

Oddly enough, this wonderful deluge of Christian material and influence could be the most detrimental thing that has ever happened to the Christian world. It heightens the possibility of complacency, lack of appreciation and spiritual boredom — and the combination of these three always opens the door to the activity of seducing spirits inside the Church.

These seducing spirits seem to have a special knack for picking up on the scent of bored believers. *False prophets and false teachers have that same knack.* That scent is like a bright shining neon sign that beckons demon spirits to come and create confusion in the Body of Christ.

Chapter Four
How To Remedy Spiritual Boredom

Knowledge without application always becomes boring and unfulfilling.

In other words, if all you do is sit and listen to the Word — and never apply it — you will reach a point of *over-saturation*. This is when boredom begins to settle into your life.

How do you remedy spiritual boredom? Do you look for something to give you a "new boost?" Do you try to find a new teaching to stir up your intellectual curiosity? Do you seek to have another new supernatural experience?

Of course it is *good* to grow in your knowledge of God's Word. It is always *good* to have new encounters with the supernatural ability of God. However, even the best teaching does *not* remedy spiritual boredom. Neither are supernatural experiences a permanent cure for this spiritual condition. Though wonderful and needed, these only delay boredom.

A wrong response to boredom in the Church will always result in a worse situation than the one which already exists. God's Word was not given just for the sake of listening, but also for the sake of "doing." It is the "doing" of the Word that removes boredom.

Applying What We have Heard

This is why James said, "Be ye doers of the Word, and

not hearers only, deceiving your own selves" (James 1:22).

The fleshly tendency, after being inundated with the Word like this over a period of time, is to sit back and become a "discusser" of the Word. You can sit there and share about all the great meetings you've attended, the famous ministers you've heard speak and can even report about all the supernatural things which you have personally observed.

Another evangelist, another miracle, another message, another teacher, another prophet. . . .

If these messages and the preached Word are not applied to your life immediately, they will probably become just another tidbit of information to add to your already growing wealth of knowledge.

Thus the reason we must "be doers of the Word, and not hearers only. . . ."

Notice especially James' usage of the phrase "hearers only." This is from the Greek word *akroates* (a-kro-a-tes) and was used in a technical sense to describe people who attended a class, not for credit, but for audit. In other words, they weren't really there to get credit for it, they were simply present to hear the lecture, think about it and then later discuss it with their friends.

These "hearers only" loved special speakers. Sometimes they would actually follow their favorite speakers from city to city. They did this because the speaker was enjoyable to hear; they liked his or her sense of humor; or they just needed *something to do*. It was fun and popular to follow some of these special speakers around.

In addition to being entertaining, sometimes these speakers could be *intellectually stimulating*. Though they had no intentions of doing anything practical with what they heard, these newly acquired tidbits of information made them look educated and all-knowing in the eyes of their peers.

Since this is the background for "hearers only" used in James 1:22, it confronts us with two important questions: *1) Are we serious about the Word of God and it's application in our lives, or 2) Are we simply "auditors" who have no intention of "doing the Word?"* Are we attending because it is the most convenient, acceptable and popular thing to do at the moment, or because our new knowledge makes us look deep and spiritual to others?

There are many people who attend church regularly, go to special meetings, read books and listen to teaching tapes. And though they have seen a lot, heard a lot and know a lot, they do nothing with the knowledge they have acquired. For them, every new message is nothing more than an intellectual exercise to fulfill their curiosity for more information.

However deep and special these tidbits of information may be, they *do not* make a person deeper or more spiritual. Only when those facts are *applied* and *acted out* in one's life do they exert spiritual power.

This is why James commanded us, "Be ye doers of the Word. . . ." The whole idea of the verse is, "Don't listen to the Word just for the sake of intellectual curiosity. Instead, do your best to practically make it work in your life after you've heard it."

James actually uses the word "doers," which comes from the Greek word *poietes* (poi-e-tes). It is from this same Greek word that we derive the title "poet."

Therefore, the word *poietes* ("doers") carries with it a sense of creative ability, *like a poet who has a creative flare in his or her life.*

By using this word, James tells us we must find "creative ways to do" the Word that has been preached and taught to us. If we cannot readily think of a practical way to "do" the Word, then we must be *creative* and *find ways* to "do" the Word.

If, however, we receive the Word just for the sake of knowledge or intellectual curiosity, we are above all others, *deceived*. This is why James continues to say, "Be ye doers of the Word, and not hearers only, *deceiving your own selves. . . .*"

Self-Deception Begins with a Wrong Concept

Spiritual maturity cannot be measured by the number of meetings we have attended, how many speakers we have heard or how much Bible knowledge we possess.

James tell us if we judge ourselves only by what we have heard and know, then we are "deceiving" ourselves. The word "deceiving" is from the Greek word *paralogidzomai* (pa-ra-lo-gid-zo-mai).

The idea of *paralogidzomai* is "miscalculation." It was first used at an early date to illustrate a librarian who compared documents, and after making the comparisons, made conclusions about these documents that were *erroneous*. His evaluation was *sincere, but wrong*. He had "misjudged, misreckoned" and made a "fallacious decision."

Because James uses this word in this context, it tells us that some people "misjudge, misreckon and miscalculate" what the "doing" of the Word really is. Some deceive themselves into wrongly thinking that *hearing* is the equivalent of *doing*.

By showing up, for example, at a Sunday service to hear the Word of God preached, they think they have "done" their responsibility for the week. James implies, "Your reasoning is full of fallacy. Your responsibility begins only after you've heard the Word."

The Word was never meant to be an intellectual game to satisfy our need for information, knowledge or curiosity. This is the "itching ears" syndrome which eventually opens the door to the deception of seducing spirits and doctrines of demons.

Paul clearly forecast this problem when he wrote,

"For the time will come when they will not endure sound doctrine; but after their own lusts shall they heap to themselves teachers, having itching ears; and they shall turn away their ears from the truth, and shall be turned unto fables" (Second Timothy 4:3-4).

Enter: False Prophets and False Teachers

This is why First Timothy 4:1 says, "Now the Spirit speaketh expressly, that in the latter times some shall depart from the faith, giving heed to seducing spirits and doctrines of demons."

In this verse, Paul describes the operation of demon spirits to lure believers away from "the faith." No sincere believer becomes involved with this type of demonic activity deliberately.

Therefore, it is safe to assume that these seducing spirits are offering these now bored, stuck-in-a-rut believers something that looks spiritual, perhaps sounds deep, profound and mystical, and may be the very thing they are looking for to reinvigorate their spiritual lives.

The truth is, if these dear believers would simply begin "doing" what they already know to do, a fresh anointing of God's Spirit would be released into their lives. *The power and anointing of God belongs to the obedient, not simply to the informed.*

Many people have a great wealth of knowledge, but no power. The power belongs to those who "do" what the Word has instructed them to do. It belongs to those who are *obedient* to God's Word. If we would all obey what we already know, that obedience would release power like we have never known in our generation.

Not realizing this very basic truth that the power belongs to those who obey and "do the Word," the Bible says "some shall depart from the faith, giving heed to seducing spirits and doctrines of demons."

43

To "depart from the faith" in order to find greater supernatural experiences, more wisdom or even higher revelation, emphatically is the work of seducing spirits. There is no doubt that this is the work of the devil to offer immature believers error in the guise of a deeper spirituality. As you shall see in the chapters to come, this is *not* the way to obtain power; this is the way *to lose power!*

We are warned in Hebrews 13:9 about being preoccupied with odd, curious, outlandish, fantastic and out-of-the-way teachings. Hebrews 13:9 says, "Be not carried about with divers and strange doctrines. For it is a good thing that the heart be established with grace; not with meats which have not profited them that have been occupied therein."

Yet, according to the Holy Spirit's prophetic warning in First Timothy 4:1, some will give heed (i.e., become preoccupied and consumed with) divers and strange doctrines in the last seasons of the Church Age.

To make absolutely certain we understand where these divers and strange doctrines come from, the Holy Spirit says, "giving heed to seducing spirits and doctrines of demons."

Chapter Five
Earnestly Contending
for the Faith

Even before the New Testament scriptures were finished being written by the apostles, the devil was already attempting to invade the Church very slowly, seductively and methodically with false prophets and false teachers who were smuggling gross *spiritual error* into the Church.

Paul, Peter, John and Jude all dealt with this false prophet, false teacher problem head-on and fearlessly when they wrote their epistles. Even at this very early time, they were aware of a spiritual attack on the gospel and knew "the faith" was in jeopardy of being *twisted, distorted and perverted.*

The seducing spirits Paul prophesied about in First Timothy 4:1, were already beginning to creep into the mainstream of the Church through the mystifying ministries of men who came with strange revelations and extremely odd supernatural activity.

Confronting a Crisis in the Church

The situation was so *critical* and had *escalated* so fast, that Jude wrote, "Beloved, when I gave all diligence to write unto you of the common salvation, it was needful for me to write you, and exhort you that ye should earnestly contend for the faith which was once delivered unto the saints" (Jude 3).

Especially notice the first part of the verse, "Beloved, when I gave all diligence to write unto you of the common salvation. . . ."

According to these opening remarks from Jude, his prior plan had been to write a pastoral epistle regarding "the common salvation" of the saints. Seeing that he was now an old man and knew that he would soon die, he wanted to leave an encouraging letter about salvation with the saints after his departure.

However, his plans to do so were interrupted by *bad news*. News had apparently just come to him that false prophets and false teachers were *infiltrating* the Church. How he received this news is not known, though some have speculated that Jude may have just received the second letter of Peter, and was stirred to action because of Peter's vivid description of false ministries in Second Peter, chapter two.

Regardless of how he heard the news, he was so *alarmed* about this problem, that he *abandoned* his original plans to write a beautiful letter about "the common salvation" and wrote another, very different letter, instead.

In this new letter, the Book of Jude, he wastes no time before he deals with the issue at hand. Right from the outset of the letter *he attacks the false ministers hard and strong, dealing to them one death blow after another, and even prophesying their final damnation.* In his letter, he stirs the saints to action — commanding them to deal with this infiltration of false prophets and false teachers bravely.

To his readers, Jude says, ". . .it was needful for me to write you. . . ." The word "needful" is the Greek word *anagke* (a-nag-ke), which denotes "a compulsion" or "a necessity." By using this special word, Jude lets us know that the problem was *urgent*.

The fact that Jude uses this word *"anagke"* means something was happening that was so insidious, that Jude felt "pressed to write" as fast as possible. *Anagke* ("needful") conveys the idea of "urgency" or the idea of a "pressing matter." Therefore, the word "needful" implies, "Because of the urgency of the moment, I was compelled and felt it absolutely imperative. . . ."

The issues that concerned Jude were so serious, he didn't feel he had the time to leisurely respond to them. He had to act immediately on the news he had received. Without hesitation, and as quickly as possible, he knew his most important task at hand was to alert the saints to the foreboding danger around them, and to spiritually instruct them on how to deal with the problem.

In view of this awesome responsibility, Jude says, ". . .it was needful to write unto you, and to exhort you. . . ."

This Means "War!"

Right from the start of his epistle, Jude lets his intentions be known. He begins using *militaristic language* to convey to his readers how intense the battle with false prophets and false teachers can become. By using this language, it is obvious that Jude wanted to declare an all out "war" on these ministers who were abusing the saints.

It is also interesting to note that Jude does not differentiate between those who are outright liars in the pulpit, those that are simply spiritually ignorant, or those that are spiritually misled.

It is emphatically clear that many of the false prophets and false teachers of the New Testament at one time had been pure in heart. When Paul refers to troublemakers and calls them by name, he nearly always refers to people whom he had ministered with at some previous point in his own ministry, or, who had at some prior time held a prominent position within the local assembly.

It is impossible to weigh the motives of a man's heart. Only God knows what lurks below the flesh. Therefore, regardless of the reason for their activities, whether from *pure motives* or *impure motives* — Jude simply sticks to the outward issues at hand and to the fruit of their ministries.

The word "exhort" is the word *parakaleo* (pa-ra-ka-leo). It means "to urge, beseech, beg" or "to encourage."

It is amazing that Jude would use this word at this point in his letter. The word *parakaleo* ("exhort") was often used by military leaders, specifically commanding officers, before they sent their troops into battle.

Rather than hide from the painful reality of war, the commanding officer would summon his troops together and would speak straightforwardly with them about the potential dangers of the battlefield. The reality of intense bloodshed, injury, danger, death and destruction was directly ahead of them.

Rather than ignore these clear-cut dangers, their commanding officer "urged, exhorted, beseeched, begged and pleaded" with the troops to *stand tall, throw their shoulders back, look the enemy straight-on — eyeball-to-eyeball, and to face their battle bravely.*

Now Jude uses this same militaristic tone of voice. From the bad news he has received, he knows that fear is attempting to invade his troops — the Church.

There was no doubt about it, a messy, messy, ugly war was developing right inside the Church between truth and error. Shutting their eyes and pretending the problem wasn't there, would not remedy the conflict. A horribly ugly war was brewing as false prophets and false teachers began to pervert the gospel with *deviant revelations.*

Therefore, rather than allowing these "enemies of the cross" (Philippians 3:18) to roam freely in and out of the Church with their damnable teachings, like an older and seasoned commanding officer, Jude takes the lead and "urges, exhorts, beseeches, pleads" and "encourages" his troops to stand strong in the brazen face of opposition.

Like it or not, they were looking straight into the face of war. The enemy had invaded their ranks through false ministries. For them, it was either *fight* for the truth of the gospel, or *surrender* to these fraudulent ministry gifts.

The false prophets and false teachers had fought long

and hard to get a foothold inside the leadership of the Church. They were not going to give up their place of notoriety easily. Therefore, Jude encourages his readers to face this undesirable situation with faith, and to confront these false ministries with boldness and courage.

Is History Repeating Itself?

To some extent, this spiritual predicament is being duplicated in the Church again today. Just as the Holy Spirit said it would occur in the "latter times," the activity of seducing spirits and doctrines of demons is attempting to enter into the mainstream of the Church.

The fact that ministers with wrong motives are active today, just as they were in the New Testament times, must not shove us backward into a fear or isolation mode. Rather, we must take a sound, reasonable, *Biblical approach* to this problem.

It is still impossible to weigh the motives of a man's heart. Therefore, rather than try to judge the unseen, secret intention of the heart, we must deal with *outward fruit*. It is possible for a ministry gift with the marks of deception on his or her ministry, to inwardly have *pure motives*.

Perhaps he or she is simply ignorant of what the Bible teaches; or perhaps he or she honestly believes that they have received a valid message for the Church. *Only God knows these things.*

Most pastors could verify that the people who have caused error and division in their churches are normally *very sincere* and honestly believe they have some kind of "word from the Lord" that validates their behavior.

A Prophetic Fruit Test

This is why Jesus told us to weigh *the fruit and not the hidden motive of the heart.*

He said, "Beware of false prophets, which come to you

in sheep's clothing, but inwardly they are ravenous wolves. *Ye shall know them by their fruits.* Do men gather grapes of thorns, or figs of thistles?"

When a traveling apostle, prophet, evangelist or teacher passes through a local vicinity, it is not possible to know them well enough to discern the intention or motive of their heart — unless this person has come through many times and now you know them well. Even then, it is not always possible to know what is truly taking place deep inside the heart.

This is why the Lord told us to watch their outward fruit! He continued to say, "Even so every good tree bringeth forth good fruit; but a corrupt tree bringeth forth bad fruit. . . Wherefore, by their fruits ye shall know them" (Matthew 7:17, 20).

In fact, this outward fruit test is so correct and precise that Jesus said, " . . .ye shall *know* them."

The word "know" is the Greek word *epiginosko* (epi-gi-no-sko). The word *epiginosko* describes an "accurate knowledge" or a "exact knowledge." Therefore, Jesus says by examining the outward fruit of a ministry, you may determine with *exact and accurate knowledge* whether or not a ministry is good or bad.

Is their message in agreement with the teaching of scripture? Does it line up with the Word, or is their message some new, unfounded revelation never before recorded in God's Word?

What does it produce in the congregation? Rebellion? Arrogance? Pride? An unhealthy independence and resistance of authority? Or does it produce the fruit of the Spirit — "love, joy, peace, longsuffering, gentleness, goodness, faithfulness, meekness and temperance" (Galatians 5:22-23)?

Does this ministry undergird the work of the local church? Or does it draw people away from the church and make them feel that church commitment isn't necessary?

Does their ministry undergird and support the authority

of the local church leadership? Or does it tear the leadership down? To whom does their new revelation draw attention — to themselves, or to the Lord?

The inward motives may not be readily known. The outward fruit, however, is very easy to determine. For this cause, Jesus told us to judge fruit — *not method, not style, not personality, not their hearts* — but fruit! "By their fruits ye shall know them," Jesus said.

Contending for the Faith

Jude continues to say, " . . .that ye should *earnestly contend* for the faith that was once delivered unto the saints."

The phrase "earnestly contend" is from the Greek word *epagonidzesthai* (ep-a-go-nid-zes-thai). What a dramatic word to describe the conflict between false prophets, false teachers and the truth!

Now Jude stops speaking in militaristic terms, and switches to *athletic terminology*. The word "earnestly contend" is a compound word that was used in a technical sense to describe the "struggle, effort, exertion" and "fighting" between two committed and determined athletes.

The second half of the word is the Greek word *agonidzo* (a-go-nid-zo). This is where we derive the word "agony." It would have been sufficient to use this word *agonidzo* alone, by itself, to convey the idea of *fighting*.

However, because Jude wants to dramatically emphasize the *intensity* of this conflict between false prophets, false teachers and the truth, he adds the prefix *ep* to the front of the word — *which gives a much stronger force and a greater sense of urgency to the matter.*

By using the total word, *epagonidzesthai*, Jude delivers a clear, unmistakable message! This conflict he is describing is not a minor disagreement over method, style, personality or opinion. This conflict is an "earnest contending," or "an intense fight and bitter struggle to the end."

Necessary Confrontations

By "urging, exhorting, beseeching, begging" and "pleading" with his readers to "earnestly contend for the faith," Jude does not mean we should involve ourselves in a mud-slinging, earthy, nasty attack upon individuals. This is the behavior of flesh and carnal weapons, and *not* the behavior of the Spirit of God or spiritual weapons.

But neither does he tell his readers to act sheepishly and timidly when it comes to defending the truth. We are commanded to hold onto truth firmly, and to refuse to allow anyone — anyone at all — regardless of how deep or spiritual they may claim to be — to draw us away from the foundational truth of the Word of God.

We must not be afraid of confrontation when confrontation is necessary. There is no need for us to go digging up confrontations either. Enough problems will arise without you having to go and find them. If the need arises and a falsehood must be confronted, then do it.

The word *epagonidzesthai* leaves no room for us to misunderstand what he is saying to us. Dealing with false prophets and false teachers is an "agonizing ordeal" that must be done bravely and in the power of the Spirit.

Chapter Six
Is Love Really Blind?

One notable minister recently said to me, "Rick, by teaching people to look at the fruit of our ministries, you're putting us on the spot... Don't you realize you're causing people to think twice before they receive our new revelations... Why would you teach these verses from the Bible? *Don't you realize, Rick, that this is not the way that love behaves?*"

Therefore, we must come face to face with the question which he put before me: "Are we walking in love by dealing with the problem of false prophets and false teachers?" "Are we walking in love by studying these important verses from the Bible?" "Should we ignore these scriptural warnings, lest they might incriminate a leader?"

This led me to ask other questions that were related to the issue. These were questions such as: "Are we walking in love if we ignore clear-cut fruit problems in a man's ministry and leave the Church at large open to his deception?" "Are we acting in love if we let people walk right into spiritual bondage without first warning them from God's Word?"

"Are we acting in love if we sit by and watch friends get caught up in ridiculous spiritual behavior that will eventually burn them so badly that they may turn from God?"

"Is it the behavior of God's love to shut your eyes, ignore obvious problems you know are there, and just hope that things will turn out all right in the end?"

Rather than deal with these problems in a straightforward, corrective manner, the *implication* by many is you should never cast a shadow on anyone or any teaching.

"In order to truly walk in love," they say, "you should just hold tight, be quiet and pray that things will work out." In other words, to these people, *"speaking the truth in love"* means to "speak nothing at all."

Certainly it is true that " . . .love covers a multitude of sins" (First Peter 4:8).

When a brother or sister, or spiritual leader has fallen into sin, we who are "spiritual" are commanded to "restore such an one in the spirit of meekness; considering thyself, lest thou also be tempted" (Galatians 6:1).

As long as the fallen leader is repentant and willing to be restored, this is our redemptive role before God.

Calling a Spade, a Spade

But what about those who refuse to change, refuse to submit, refuse to heed counsel, and refuse to believe that they are wrong in any of their actions or teachings, and are accountable to no one at all?

These belligerent individuals, who may dress up their belligerency in the disguise of "boldness," are usually beyond a peaceful restoration by virtue of their *own decision* to go their *own way.*

In such cases in the New Testament, the apostles were not afraid to be blunt or to call the shots as they saw them. They called a spade, a spade, never apologized once for having a strong opinion about a matter, never flinched once when false prophets and false teachers accused them of a lack of love — and even called the names of their spiritual adversaries *publicly!*

Were they acting in love?

In our day this would probably be viewed as an act of malice, bitterness, contempt or even possibly viewed as a ploy to undermine someone else's ministry because of jealousy.

Because the apostles loved and cherished the Church so much, they understood they had *a responsibility to the flock.* To allow fraudulent ministers to come in and take advantage of the flock with no warning, would be anything *except* an act of love.

Speaking "the truth in love" to them meant they must "guard the flock over which the Holy Spirit had made them overseers" (Acts 20:28). What an awesome responsibility!

Realizing this great responsibility, they challenged, rebuked and flatly spoke the plain truth about these matters with no regrets. Why? In order to protect the larger body from insidious men who were worming their ways into prominent positions in the Church.

In First Timothy 1:20, Paul "spoke the truth in love" when he publicly stated that two well-known leaders, Hymenaeus and Alexander, had been "delivered over to Satan that they may learn not to blaspheme."

Was this an act of love?

Was it right to tell the whole Church about this disciplinary action, thus causing embarrassment for Hymenaeus and Alexander? Emphatically "yes!" This powerful statement from the apostle Paul alerted the Church to the *detrimental fruit* of these men's ministries! There is no question about it, *this was an act of love.*

In Second Timothy 2:16, Paul commands Timothy to "shun profane and vain babbling...." In the following verse, verse 17, he goes so far in his warning as to *specifically reveal* who these "profane and vain babblers" were! He says, "And their word will eat as doth a canker; of whom is Hymenaeus and Philetus...."

Was this an act of love?

Was it correct to publicly name these men and even to go so far as to call them "cankers?" Was this the right thing to do? Though this seems to be unduly hard, the answer is absolutely "yes!"

This was love warning a congregation and a young preacher, in the strongest of terms, to stay away from these bitter and back-slidden men who would spiritually hurt them.

In Second Timothy 4:10, Paul announces to the whole Christian world of the day that one of his former associates, Demas, had forsaken him. In Second Timothy 4:14, he states again that Alexander (the same Alexander he delivered to Satan in First Timothy 1:20) was still unrepentant and not worthy of trust.

In Third John, verses 9 and 10, the Apostle John (the apostle of "love") clearly tells his readers that a spiritual leader named Diotrephes was *a troublemaker and was preoccupied with his own bloated sense of self-importance.*

Was this kind of straightforward talk really "speaking the truth in love?" *"Yes, yes, yes, emphatically, yes!"*

Love Says, "Be Careful of Danger!"

Let me put it to you like this: "If you saw a child running into a busy street that had tens of cars driving past at great speeds, would it be love to let that child run right out into that street?" Of course not! You would shout as *loud* as you could to get that child's attention and stop him from death.

At that precarious moment, real love would not gently whisper "please be careful." Instead, real love would *scream, holler and yell as loud as it could!* Love would act fast, hard and immediately.

Bystanders who didn't see the dangerous situation as closely as you did, may misunderstand and accuse you of being "too harsh" or "unkind" when calling out to the child. However, the *bottom-line* is you got the attention of the child and saved him from death.

For this same reason, *Jude speaks loudly about the false*

prophet and false teacher issue. If he only sighs a faint whisper about this problem, no one will hear him or realize the critical nature of the situation.

Therefore, he raises his voice like the voice of a commander and urges his readers to march forward to war against the heretics in the Church!

Make no Bones about It!

When Paul wrote about the ministries of false prophets and false teachers, he made no bones about letting his feelings about them be known! He was so thoroughly convinced of their evil and insidious nature, that he went so far as to call them "dogs" (Philippians 3:2).

Those are strong sentiments, aren't they? Why were his feelings about false prophets and false teachers so strong? Because he knew that these evil workers — *like mad, rabid dogs* — were viciously ripping apart the Word of God — they were altering it, they were tearing it to pieces, they were dismembering it — they were destroying the foundations of "the faith" that the apostles had labored to lay in place.

Paul was so convinced of the evil-hearted condition of these sinister ministers, that he describes them as individuals who were "taken captive" by the devil, to do the devil's will (Second Timothy 2:26).

The word "captive" is from the word *zoogreo* (zoo-gre-o), and it refers to the act of "catching a wild animal and taking it alive into captivity." This is where we get the word "zoo."

In using such terminology, Paul means to tell us that rebellious spiritual leaders who are unrepentant about their ways and who refuse to base their ministries on the Word of God, eventually become so raving mad and wild in their spiritual approach to things, that they become like a wild and dangerous animal.

Biblical Terminology for Sinister Ministers

The New Testament writers had no problem expressing their sentiments about false ministers. Their descriptions of them were dramatic, pointed and derogatory.

It is interesting to note that the New Testament writers never gave detailed explanations or job descriptions for the real gifts. However, they were sure to record their thoughts about the false!

Because the apostles wanted to alert the people to the danger of these sinister ministers, they stated their warnings in the most powerful words possible.

Let's see how Paul describes false prophets and false teachers. He says they are:

— "deceitful workers" (Second Corinthians 11:13).

— a "thorn in the flesh" and "a messenger of Satan" (Second Corinthians 12:7).

— troublemakers (Galatians 1:7).

— "false brethren" (Galatians 2:4).

— refers to them as "witches" (Galatians 3:1).

— "dogs" and "evil workers" (Philippians 3:2).

— "enemies of the cross" (Philippians 3:18).

— "beguilers" (Colossians 2:4, 18).

— refers to them as "spoilers" (Colossians 2:8).

— "vain janglers" (First Timothy 1:6).

— "liars" with "seared consciences" (First Timothy 4:2).

— "proud" and "know nothing" and are "full of envy, strife, railings and evil surmisings" (First Timothy 6:4).

— they have "corrupt minds and are "destitute of the truth" (First Timothy 6:5).

— "profane and vain babblers" (Second Timothy 2:16).

— vividly describes them as "cankers" (Second Timothy 2:17).

— they are "taken captive by the devil" to do the devil's will (Second Timothy 2:26).

— "evil men and seducers" (Second Timothy 3:13).

— they are "unruly, vain talkers" and "deceivers" (Titus 1:10).

— they are "subverters" (Titus 1:11).

— "liars, evil beasts, slow bellies" (Titus 1:12).

— and they are "heretics" (Titus 3:10).

This is how the Apostle Paul referred to these sinister minsters. Now, let's move beyond Paul to see how Peter described these individuals who masqueraded as spiritual leaders.

— Peter says they are "false prophets and false teachers" (Second Peter 2:1).

— they are controlled by "covetousness"; they speak "feigned words"; and are spiritual "merchandisers" (Second Peter 2:3).

— they "walk after the flesh in the lust of uncleanness" (Second Peter 2:10).

— they "despise authorities"; they are "presumptuous, headstrong, brazen and rude"; they are "self-willed"; and they "malign dignities" (Second Peter 2:10).

— "natural brute beasts" that are "made to be taken and destroyed" (Second Peter 2:12).

— they are "spots" and "blemishes" in our love feasts (Second Peter 2:13).

— they have "eyes of adultery, that cannot cease from sin" (Second Peter 2:14).

— "cursed children" (Second Peter 2:14).

— they have "forsaken the right way, and are gone astray, following the way of Balaam" (Second Peter 2:15).

— vividly calls them "wells without water" and

"clouds that are carried about with a tempest" (Second Peter 2:17).

— they are themselves "the servants of corruption" (Second Peter 2:19).

— they have become "entangled" in the "pollutions of the world" again (Second Peter 2:20).

— though they once were pure in heart, they have "turned from the holy commandment" (Second Peter 2:21).

— And finally, Peter likens them to a "dog turned to his own vomit" and "a sow that was washed to her wallowing in the mire" (Second Peter 2:22).

Then we come to Jude's graphic portrayal of these false ministers. Jude declares that they are:

"Ungodly men" (verse 4); "filthy dreamers, despisers of authority, and verbal assaulters of dignities" (verse 9); "brute beasts" (verse 10); "spots in your love feasts, clouds without water, carried about of winds; trees whose fruit withereth, without fruit; twice dead, plucked up by the roots" (verse 12); "raging waves of the sea, foaming out of their own shame; wandering stars" (verse 13); "murmurers, complainers, walking after their own lusts; speaking great swelling words; having men's persons in admiration because of advantage" (verse 16); "mockers" and "sensual" (verses 18-20).

Seeing this was the terminology which the apostles used to describe false prophets and false teachers, it is no small wonder that Paul indicated that they can become so raving mad and wild in their spiritual approach to things, *that they almost become like a wild, rabid, dangerous animal*!

From One Excess to the Next Excess

As you shall see in the pages to follow in this chapter, one level of excess always leads to the next. *If your spiritual foundation is off-base and wrong, then your entire spiritual structure will be off-base and wrong.*

Over the passing of time, a person who is constantly pre-occupied with off-base beliefs, outlandish teachings and truly weird new revelations, will lose his or her *usefulness* as a working member in the Body of Christ.

An off-base believer or minister can become so driven and determined to have another higher experience, then another and another, that they eventually lose touch with reality altogether. Christianity to them is a "goose bump" or a "cloud" that floats by.

Thus, because they are so far removed from reality around them, they lose their basic usefulness to the kingdom of God.

This reminds me of one particular group who claimed to be in pursuit of greater revelation and more of the Spirit's power. With *real sincerity* of heart and a genuine, deep love for the Lord, their pursuit of a greater spirituality and more power began.

First, they moved over into *extreme forms* of intercession. Out of a pure desire to experience more of God and His power, they begin to do things in the natural which they had been taught would produce supernatural power in their lives and ministries.

Clutching their stomachs as tightly as they could, and bearing down upon their abdomens as though they were in intense pain and were about to "give birth" to a baby, they hollered and screamed violently at the top of their lungs in other tongues, as they fell down onto the ground.

They had been wrongly taught that this outward, physical behavior and violent screaming was a new form of intercession that would somehow cause them to "press in" to the realm of the spirit, where they would be able to "give birth" to things in the spirit realm.

This teaching on intercession became so profoundly out-of-balance, that in time, they appointed "spiritual midwives" to rub the bodies of intercessors and to help them relax as they "birthed" things spiritually. Lying on the floor and pushing downward for hours with all of the strength they could muster, they attempted to gain new territory in the spirit realm for the kingdom of God.

Certainly there is a genuine "travail" in prayer. I have experienced this "travail" of the spirit in my own personal prayer life.

However, there is no scriptural precedent for believing that this "travail" is something that we bring about by ourselves; there is no precedent in scripture that says we must bear down upon our abdomens as though we are having babies when we pray; and there is no scriptural precedent for believing that "spiritual midwives" are needed to bring forth genuine intercession.

Even as I write, I am reminded of a church in Lincoln, Illinois, where I have observed beautiful, balanced and powerful "travail." There is no doubt that there is a genuine "travail" in the spirit.

However, it wasn't long until this excessive and error-ridden understanding of intercession led to *another level of spiritual excess.* To be truly set free from Satan's control over their lives, they taught that Christians must go through a measure of *daily deliverance* from demon spirits.

It wasn't long until this group became viewed by many as the "barf-bag" church. Week after week, they were instructed to deliver themselves of demons by vomiting and coughing those demons out of their bodies!

Then they moved into their third and absolutely incredible level of spiritual excess: *baby intercession!*

"Since babies are born pure," they said, "with no sin or guile in their spirits, they should be able to pray perfectly and with great power."

Therefore, when infants cried during their worship services, they were instructed to let them lay there and cry. Why? Because this was supposedly "their spirits crying out in intercession to God."

This, dear friend, is spiritual insanity!

In order to keep a balanced perspective of things, when a new, exciting teaching comes around, ask yourself: "Can I see Jesus doing this?" "Can I see the apostles sitting around and taking part in this kind of activity?"

If your answer is "no," or if there is a hesitation in your spirit, then you should know that you're dealing with something that is possibly out-of-balance and unscriptural.

Can you see the apostle Paul, seated in a circle with Peter and John, and all three of them lying on their backs, pushing downward upon their abdomens, and screaming violently in other tongues as though they were experiencing the agonizing pains of giving birth to a baby?

Do you think Paul ever practiced this kind of prayer?

Can you imagine Paul calling for "spiritual midwives" to come and rub his body, and to help him physically relax, so that he could give birth to these spiritual things a little easier?

Absolutely not!

This was the kind of error that Paul was trying to correct inside the Church! It may be true that he "travailed" in prayer from time to time (Galatians 4:19). But this is taking it one step too far! He never even begins to insinuate that he did these physical, outward things in order to get spiritual results.

A good rule of thumb for sensible Charismatic Christianity is: "Would Jesus, Paul or any of the other apostles do this?" "Is there any *Biblical precedent* or *principle* for this kind of activity in the book of Acts?"

Commendation for Sincerity

The sad thing about this is, people who strongly follow this type of spirituality are normally *very sincere and genuinely hungry for God.* They are to be *commended* for their spiritual hunger and willingness to pursue God's power.

However, because they have never been afforded a sound scriptural foundation, or have rejected it for the sake of "deeper things," they are now headed in a dangerous direction that will open them up to the supernatural activity of demon spirits and error of the worst kind.

A revelation that goes "beyond the Bible" isn't worth one minute of your day.

The off-base revelations I am writing about have nothing to do with the gifts of the Spirit. Of course we need the revelation gifts of the Holy Spirit in the Church today. These marvelous gifts of the Holy Spirit will be with us until Jesus comes again.

However, revelatory gifts of the Spirit such as the "word of knowledge," the "word of wisdom," "discerning of spirits," "prophecy" and "interpretation of tongues" primarily operate within the Church for the sake of personal ministry, and not for the sake of doctrine or teaching.

For example, a dear friend in the ministry recently wrote me and related the following story about how God used the gift of "the word of knowledge" to set a woman free from years of bondage.

My friend related how a very large, obese woman with many medical problems had come forward for prayer at the end of a church service. When the minister stepped forward to pray for this dear woman, the Holy Spirit gave a "word of knowledge" like my friend had never heard before.

The Holy Spirit instructed my minister friend, "Tell this afflicted woman to drink 10 glasses of distilled water with lemon juice mixed in it for three days. Then, for the next seven days, tell her to eat fruit and vegetables. After this, she must return to drinking distilled water with lemon juice mixed with it for another seven days. . . And see if I won't restore her health."

My friend told me, "I argued with the Lord about giving

this word, because it sounded so strange to me. However, I finally obeyed and gave her the word which the Lord had spoken to me."

After the word was given, my friend was told that this woman was a diabetic, and had been on insulin for 10 years.

Realizing the serious nature of this woman's medical condition, she asked the pastor to come forward. With the pastor standing at the side of the afflicted woman, my friend instructed the woman to follow her pastor's advice in regard to her diet, and that if any strange physical symptoms started to act up, she should do what her pastor said.

As my friend continued the story, she said, "About two months later, the woman who had been overweight and had been sick, drove 250 miles to see us. I hardly recognized her. She had lost 50 pounds and looked fantastic. She was off insulin and her blood sugar was normal. She was made whole."

You may wonder why I'm relating this story to you. It's because in this particular example you cannot find a precedent or "formula" in the Word for receiving healing in this way. Yet, it perfectly depicts how the "word of knowledge" and the gifts of healing work within the framework of the Church. God does these supernatural and awesome things in His own way.

This technically was a "revelation" that was new. In other words, you're not going to find that same word from the Lord contained anywhere in scripture. Yet, it was correct.

Then what do I mean when I refer to revelations that go "beyond the Bible?"

By "beyond the Bible," I mean to refer to those visions, dreams, teachings and revelations that are so far-fetched that they cannot be linked to any previous *scriptural precedent* or to *the spirit of scripture.* They confirm no scripture, agree with no scripture, or perhaps are even diametrically opposed to some principle in the Word.

If you pursue this way-out approach to spiritual things, like others who have pursued this course of action before you, neither will you be fit for service in the kingdom of God.

People who are given over to this approach of spirituality, normally cannot receive correction and in fact, may feel "persecuted" when someone does try to help them see the error of their ways.

This unwarranted sense of persecution drives them even closer into their little tightly-knit group, until finally, they become so unbalanced that they believe no one is right, except their little group.

To believe you possess a piece of special revelation that is higher and better than anyone else's, is the height of spiritual arrogance!

False prophets and false teachers prey on people with intense spiritual desire. Especially during lulls in the Church, when God's power seems to be dormant, these fraudulent ministers appear on the scene with all kinds of revelations to provide a *psuedo-spirituality* for those who want to move on with God.

Chapter Seven
Beating the Dogs Off
of the Faith

Devastation was written all across the pastor's face that day, as he opened his heart and began to tell me about a terrible experience he had recently had with a visiting speaker.

"We were thrilled when we heard that he had agreed to come and minister in our church," he told me. "Really, we were shocked that he was going to come here to be with us. I immediately asked the church family to start praying for a mighty outpouring of God's power upon the meetings."

"Months later," he continued, "when he arrived for the meetings, I had no idea that a horrible scene was about to occur. It simply devastated me to see and hear what he did in my own pulpit," the pastor added.

I was grieved to hear what the traveling speaker had done to this pastor and his congregation. In a mere matter of four days, this church family had been ripped to pieces by the man whom they had invited to come and "bless" them.

As he continued to tell me the story, he related how the speaker had told the congregation, "Your pastor doesn't have the guts to tell you what I'll tell you. It takes boldness and courage to speak up and say it the way it really is. Your pastor simply doesn't have this kind of boldness and courage in his ministry."

I asked him, "If this was the way he was behaving in your pulpit, then why did you let him continue ministering that night, and even more, why did you have him back for three additional nights? You should have cancelled the meeting and told him to go home!"

"Well," he continued, "because he is so well-known and is growing in popularity, I kept telling myself that maybe he was right. He obviously knows a lot of well-known people who endorse him. In light of this, I just kept thinking that maybe he was right."

By the time these four days of special meetings were over, this church family had been insulted, assaulted, and ripped to shreds.

The more mature members of the congregation, knowing the sincere heart of the pastor, were praying for his protection, and for the protection of the church.

On the other hand, the younger converts, because they were hungry for a move of God's power, falsely mistook his lack of respect for authority as "boldness." Unfortunately, they were drawn to him like a bug in the summer night is drawn to a bright and shining porchlight. They thronged around him and told the pastor, "this man is deep! Whew! He has a message that we really need."

This was just the beginning of trouble. After the meetings were over and the speaker had left town, many of them who were drawn to his arrogant behavior began to imitate him. Some of them even began to call themselves prophets and took him as a role model for what their prophetic ministry was supposed to be like.

When the pastor called him to discuss the trouble he left behind, he told the pastor, "It's your problem, not mine. If you were a stronger man, you'd be able to handle a ministry like mine. My anointing is obviously too heavy for you to handle."

Where did the Charismatic world ever get the idea

68

that a "heavy anointing" is rude, harsh, sarcastic and unkind?

If the anointing is extremely heavy upon a man or woman, then the gracious, Christ-like fruit of the Spirit should should be just as heavy. Even boldness should be permeated with Christ's love, compassion and tender mercies.

As he related the story to me, I was reminded of Peter's description of the wild, insane, untamed and ungodly behavior of false prophets and false teachers.

Natural Brute Beasts

According to Peter, these pseudo spiritual leaders are like "natural brute beasts, which are made to be taken and destroyed" (Second Peter 2:12).

This is strong language, isn't it? Hold on, because when you see the meaning of these words from the Greek, you'll realize just how strongly Peter felt about such individuals.

The word "natural" is from the Greek word *phusikos* (phu-si-kos). It refers to "a mere creature of instinct, like an animal that is born to be caught and eventually slaughtered." The word "brute" is from the Greek word *alogos* (a-lo-gos) and it describes "irrationality" or even better, "a lack of intelligence."

By using these carefully chosen words, Peter declares that fraudulent ministers are like "mere creatures of instinct which are led by base appetites; they have bodies, but no minds; *they are the equivalent of spiritual idiots.*"

Though this is very strong language, Peter isn't finished yet. In addition to this, he continues to tell us that false prophets and false teachers are similar to "natural, brute beasts. . . ."

The word "beasts" is from the Greek word *zoon* (pronounced zo-on), which refers once again to "animal life." It is the same root from which we have obtained the word "zoo."

When you put all of these words together, it is clear that Peter means to say, sadly, that if error-ridden ministries do not repent and come back into spiritual order, they will become like *"mere creatures of instinct who possess no common sense, are mentally vacant, and are very similar to wild, ferocious animals who belong behind bars at the zoo, or out in the wild — far away from people."*

Then Peter immediately tells us that these sinister ministers are "made to be *taken* and destroyed. . . ."

The word "taken" is taken from the word *alusis* (a-lusis), and means to "capture" or "to take something alive." It is a graphic picture of catching a terribly dangerous, wild animal to place behind bars for viewing, or perhaps on the wall as a trophy.

Peter obviously has no trouble finding words to express his thoughts about false prophets and false teachers! According to his view of things, they are so wild, untamed and deadly, that if caught, you would have obtained quite a trophy!

However, he is also is sure to let us know most of these fraudulent ministers will end up destroying themselves. For this cause, he says they are "made to be taken and *destroyed*. . . ."

This word "destroyed" is from the Greek word *phthora* (ph-tho-ra), which describes the act of "annihilation." This is exactly what dangerously wild beasts eventually will do to each other. They are territorial creatures who kill anything that tries to move in on their area.

Ultimately, like uncivilized animals, Peter says, "they shall utterly perish in their own corruption."

Beating the Dogs Off of the Faith

But according to Jude, verse 3, the false prophets and false teachers of this time were not attacking each other, but rather, they were attacking "the faith."

"The faith" was being victimized by these savage and ferocious false prophet and false teacher "dogs." Thus the reason that Jude commands his readers "to earnestly contend for the faith that was once delivered unto the saints."

The phrase "the faith" doesn't refer to raw faith, such as faith for miracles, signs and wonders or supernaturally related activity. The word "faith" is the Greek word *pistei* (pis-tei), and it is used in this context to denote the teaching of doctrine or scripture.

Therefore, the battle that was raging inside the Church was a battle over the issue of truth — *not style, method or personality* — but over "the faith." Styles, methods and personalities are always changing. This was not the issue at hand. The real issue at stake was "the faith."

Doctrine and sound teaching of the Word of God was at risk because of fraudulent ministers who were fiendishly mauling the Word and ripping it to pieces. Therefore, in light of this situation, Jude urges his readers to "earnestly contend for *the faith. . . .*"

No Improvements Needed

This "faith," Jude says, "was once for all delivered unto the saints."

The word "once" is the Greek word *apax* (a-pax), and it literally means "once for all." It carrys idea of "completion, finality," or something that is so complete that it needs nothing more to be added unto it.

By using this word *apax*, Jude clearly states the written Word doesn't need any improvements, additions or further new revelations added to it. It was delivered "once for all" — as a "finished, completed, perfect work."

The fact that he uses this word *apax* ("once for all") tells us why a battle was raging over the issue of the Word. False prophets and false teachers were attempting to add new insights, new teachings, brand new revelations, etc., to the Word.

Therefore, Jude makes his message strong and clear: This Word was given with no further need of improvement. As it stands today, this Word is "complete."

Entrusted into our Safe Keeping

To alert us to our responsbility concerning the Word and sound doctrine, Jude continues to say this faith was "once *delivered* unto the saints."

The word "delivered" is the word *paradidomi* (pa-ra-di-do-mi), and it means to "deliver over to someone; to entrust to someone for their safe keeping" or "to commit and hand down" as in a family tradition.

Traditions are easily lost. If not lost altogether, then over a period of time they can be altered and changed from one generation to the next — *unless someone cares enough about them to preserve them!*

Those faithful ones who want to keep family traditions such as Christmas traditions, New Year's traditions and Thanksgiving traditions the same year after year, are thought to be "abnormally picky" and "hard-to-get-along-with" by others, who really don't care that much about family traditions.

But these traditions would be lost and discarded altogether if it weren't for those "abnormally picky" people who fight year after year to preserve them!

By using the word "delivered," Jude sets this very example before us. He confronts his readers with their responsibility to carefully handle the Word of God and to keep it as close to the original, written form as possible.

This is the reason we read, study, and even use Hebrew and Greek as we study God's Word. Why? So we can understand the Word more clearly; know exactly what God is saying to us; and so we can impart this powerful Word in a pure, correct form to others. Our purpose is to keep this Word as close to it's original, written form as possible.

This is our responsibility before God.

The Highest Form of Revelation Available

In Second Timothy 3:16, the Apostle Paul said, "All scripture is given by inspiration of God, and is profitable for doctrine, for reproof, for correction, for instruction in righteousness; that the man of God may be perfect, thoroughly furnished unto all good works."

Notice that Paul says, "All scripture is given *by inspiration of God. . . .*"

The word "inspiration" is from the Greek word *theopneustos* (theo-pneu-stos), and is a compound of the words *theos* (the-os) and *pneuma* (pneu-ma). *Theos* is the Greek word for "God," and *pneuma* is translated as the words "breath" or "spirit."

When compounded together, they form the word *theopneustos,* which is where we get the word "inspiration." Therefore, when the Bible speaks of "inspiration" (as used in this verse), it literally portrays the picture of *God breathing His very own breath and presence into something.*

So when Paul declares, "All scripture is given by inspiration of God," he means to tell us that *the written Word actually contains within it the presence, life, breath and spirit of God.* God has literally breathed His own life and essence into this Word.

In light of this, *the written Word is the highest form of revelation that is available to man today.* While it is wonderful to have dreams and visions — and we sorely need the genuine manifestation of these in the Church today — these are not on the same level of the Word and never shall be.

According to Second Timothy 3:16, the Word actually holds the very breath of God Himself, and this powerful presence is available to anyone who will read the Word, study the Word, and pray over it. To all who seek to unlock the truths contained in this Word, God offers the

73

promise of *supernatural power.*

As Ecclesiates 8:4 has so accurately stated, *"Where the word of a king is, there is power. . . ."*

An Example of Spiritual Absurdity

This is why we must be aware of those who would try to draw us away from the consistent diet of the Word of God.

Though they may pretend to know new and better ways to obtain spiritual power, and may even come with the "appearance" of new supernatural manifestations, we must not follow their advice to abandon the Word of God in order to pursue "deeper things."

An example of this spiritual absurdity recently occurred when a minister allegedly told a large audience, "Stay away from ministers who are 'Word-bound.' They'll just 'Word you to death.'"

He allegedly continued, "If you are a member of a Church where the pastor is unduly heavy on the Word, then get out of that church and go to some other place where you can get into the flow of the supernatural."

Where is our spiritual sensibility? It should be obvious to anyone that this is the pinnacle of *spiritual foolishness.* Such statements reveal excessive ignorance concerning the Word of God and its divine nature; and if it is possible to be "Word-bound" as this particular leader has suggested, then we must pray for this marvelous spiritual condition to come upon us and *overtake us!*

The prospect of being 'Word-bound' is perhaps the best prospect man has ever known! Just think of the privilege of being overtaken and bound by the Word that contains the presence, power, breath, spirit and essence of God Himself!

Before a large, impressionable crowd, the same man has suggested (my paraphrase)," You don't need to go as deep into the Word as some of these folks are trying to take you. And you must be especially aware of those folks who go so deep that they even use Hebrew and Greek in their messages. There's no power, no anointing or value in that kind of teaching. *Stay away from it."*

The implication is that leaders, like myself and others who study the Word in its orginial text, are boring, dull and have nothing "exciting" to say to the Church.

First of all, it is *absolutely true* that some ministers are dull to listen to. I must agree. However, this has nothing to do with their strong emphasis on the Word of God, or their use of Biblical languages. This is an absurdity!

Everything we are spiritually — *right now and in the days and years to come* — is because of God's Word at work in our lives! The Bible teaches:

— We are clean through the Word (John 15:3).

— We are strengthened by the Word (Acts 20:32).

— We obtain faith from the Word (Romans 10:17).

— We are sanctified by the Word (Ephesians 5:26).

— We are commanded to take the sword of the Spirit, which is the Word of God (Ephesians 6:17).

— We are commanded to hold forth the Word of life (Philippians. 2:16).

— We are commanded to let the Word dwell in us richly (Colossians. 3:16).

— We know the Word is quick, powerful, and sharper than any two-edged sword (Hebrews 4:12).

— We understand the worlds were framed by the Word of God (Hebrews 11:3).

— We were begotten by the Word (James 1:18).

— We were born again by the Word (I Peter 1:23).

— We grow spiritually as a result of feeding on the Word (I Peter 2:2).

— We are made strong against the evil one because of the indwelling Word (I John. 2:14).

— We overcome Satan by the Word (Revelation 12:11).

How could anyone ever think or preach that they can have too much of the Word in their lives? *If you remove the work of the Word, you will remove the work of God from your life completely.*

If some preachers and teachers are boring, dull and dead, it is not because of their strong emphasis on the Bible or their use of Biblical languages. *The real issue here is anointing.*

The same man has even gone so far as to imply that the Bible was not even written in Hebrew or Greek. Rather, he says, it was "written in spirit."

What in the world does *that* mean?

According to his profoundly out-of-balance view of things, those who spend time digging, searching and studying the Word in it's original text, are out of touch with the supernatural and are wasting their time.

His undermining of the written Word has gone so far, that he has also allegedly said, "In order to obtain supernatural revelation from the Bible, you must go out into the realm of the spirit, stop depending on your natural mind, and receive your revelation knowledge *only* by supernatural means."

The problem with this kind of teaching is that it attracts the *undisciplined* and the *spiritually immature;* and it tantalizes the soul-realm into believing that you can have something for nothing.

I must absolutely agree that we need a greater demonstration of God's power in the Church today. Who wouldn't agree with this? We must be seeking God right now for a fuller release of His power upon the Church.

However, we do not abandon the Word and sound doctrine in order to obtain it. The plain truth is, though some of these leaders talk at great lengths about going out into the realm of the spirit in order to obtain this power — and publicly ridicule others for not having it — they rarely demonstrate the power of God in their own ministries.

There is a lot of talk and hype about power, but not a lot of power in action right now. We must pray for a *true release* of God's power for these days in which we live. We need a true demonstration of His power for these last days.

Waterless Wells and Spiritual Fog

Peter continues to tell us that such ministers are like "wells without water, clouds that are carried about with a tempest; to whom the mist of darkness is reserved forever" (Second Peter 2:17).

The word "wells" refers to a deep, deep well in which there is no "spring of water" to draw from. Though the well appears to be very deep, the Greek says it is *anudros* (a-nu-dros), or "waterless."

This is how Peter describes false prophets and false teachers. It seems they always claim to have fresh, deep spiritual insight; they boast of knowing what no one else knows; and often they claim to be on the front lines of a future move of God. They point their finger toward the future and spend all their time and energies talking about *the next move of God* (i.e., what it will be like, how to get ready for it, etc).

You must be very careful of those individuals who talk constantly about *the future* and have nothing practical to add to life right now. It is absolutely true that we must prepare for the next move of God's Spirit. Thank God for those specially in-tune ministers with prophetic insight, who have a knack for seeing *what God is going to do next in the Church on a major scale*. We desperately need well-grounded, established, tested, balanced prophetic ministry today.

But you must also be aware of *opportunists*. They also have a *special knack*. They know when God's people are spiritually bored. They have plugged into the truth that people have a deep-seated need for the supernatural power of God. They know that these hungry people are famished for a new outpouring of power.

This is when false revelators spring up on the scene. They take advantage of this God-given, deep-seated desire for the supernatural that is crying out from the heart of God's people.

Peter continues to call these fraudulent ministers, "*clouds* that are carried about with a tempest. . . ."

The word "clouds" is from the Greek word *homichle* (ho-mich-le), which refers to a "fog" or "mist."

By using this word, Peter declares that false prophets and false teachers may look deep, but in reality, they have no more substance than a "fog" or a "mist." In other words they are *dense*, but *empty*.

Stormy Weather

To let us know what these spiritual actors will produce in the Church if given a chance, Peter says they "are clouds carried about with *a tempest*. . . ."

The word "tempest" is from the word *lailapsi* (lai-lapsi). It describes a "storm" or a "squall" and is the very same word used in Mark 4:37 to describe the "great storm of wind" that threatened to destroy Jesus and his disciples on their way to the country of the Gadarenes. At the shores of Gadara, Jesus moved in a *supernatural power* like his disciples had never before seen!

Now Peter uses this same "stormy" word to convey what these sinister ministers will produce in the Church.

If such opportunists are allowed a place of prominence on the front lines of leadership, they will *certainly not* produce the next move of God. According to Peter, they will instead produce a *nasty, stormy, turbulent situation inside the Church.* This turbulent, spiritually ridiculous "squall" may keep us from ever reaching the shores of our own Gadara — where the next genuine move of God will bestow desperately needed *supernatrural power* upon us.

Peter also is certain to tell us that false prophets and false teachers are like "clouds that are *carried about. . . .*" This phrase "carried about" is from the Greek word *elauno* (e-lau-no) and it literally means to "blow" or to be "fiercely driven."

In this context, Peter says these fraudulent ministers are unceasing in their "drive" and "ambition" to get to the top. He or she simply does not know when to give up. They normally continue to sweep the land like a "driven wind," until at last, the storm runs out of steam and fades away — never to wreak havoc again.

Great Swelling Words of Vanity

He continues to say, "For when they speak great swelling words of vanity, they allure through the lusts of the flesh, through much wantonness, those that were clean escaped from them who live in error."

"Great swelling words of vanity" is very interesting. The phrase "great swelling words" is taken from the Greek word *huperogkos* (hu-per-og-kos), and it is used to denote something that is "swollen, boated, inflated" or "terribly exaggerated."

Fraudulent ministries use unbelievable *ostentatious verbosity* as a regular part of their delivery. In other words, they exaggerate their spirituality and have an unrealistic view of their own, special importance. They claim to be a whole lot more than they actually are!

Peter says they speak "great swelling words of *vanity.*" The word "vanity" is from the word *mataios* (ma-tai-os) and it refers to something that is "of no significance." This means that though they claim greatness, they really represent a lot of spiritual insignificance!

Also notice who this type of behavior primarily attracts! Peter says, ". . .they allure through the lusts of the flesh, through much wantonness, *those that were clean escaped from them who live in error."* In other words, they primarily attract the spiritually immature.

Notice how they lure these young believers to their message. They do it through "much wantonness." The idea of "wantonness" is "utter abandonment" or "reckless, unbridled conduct."

Some of this reckless, unbridled conduct is found several verses earlier, in verse 10. Here, Peter tells us exactly how these individuals carry on in the course of their public ministry.

In Second Peter 2:10, he says, "But chiefly them that walk after the flesh in the lust of uncleanness, and despise governments. Presumptuous are they, self-willed, they are not afraid to speak evil of dignities."

Scorning Pastors and Ridiculing Authorities

Especially pay careful attention to the fact that Peter says these error-ridden ministers "despise governments."

The word "despise" is from the Greek word *kataphroneo* (ka-ta-phro-neo), and it is a compound of the words *kata* and *phroneo*. The word *kata* means "down" and the word *phroneo* describes "the mind" or "intelligence."

When these two are compounded into one word (*kataphroneo*), they describe the act of "condescending to someone in a humiliating fashion." It is the idea of "disdaining, ridiculing, putting down, humiliating, "scorning" or "laughing at someone."

To let you know just how strong and verbally abusive this word is, this is the same word used in Mark 5:40, when the Bible tells us that "they laughed him to scorn" because Jesus likened Jairus' daughter's death to a temporary sleep.

However, notice who it is that these false ministers are humiliating, scorning and poking fun toward. The Word says they are directing all of this foul behavior toward *"governments."*

The word "governments" is from the Greek word *kuriotes* (ku-rio-tes). This *does not* refer to disrespect for the government of a nation, though sometimes they may behave this way too. The word "governments" (*kuriotes*) would be more accurately translated as the word "authorities" or "lordships."

When Jude covers this same area of ungodly behavior in his letter (Jude 8-11), he makes it absolutely clear who these troublemakers are *attacking verbally.*

In Jude, verse 11, he says, "Woe to them! For they have gone in the way of Cain, and ran greedily after the error of Balaam for reward, and perished in the gainsayings of Korah."

In this important verse, we discover that Jude likens the behavior of these false ministries to three different individuals: 1) *Cain,* 2) *Balaam,* and 3) *Korah.* In all three of these cases, *the real sin was rebellion and a lack of respect for authority.*

Cain rebelled against the authority of God; Balaam had absolutely no respect for the authority of God; *and Korah had no respect for Moses, who was God's designated authority over Israel.*

In light of this insight from Jude, when Peter declares false ministers "despise governments," he is clearly telling us that false prophets and false teachers have *utter contempt* for those who are in authority.

Because Jude ends with the example of Korah, who fatally tried to come against the authority of Moses, he is pointing out the fact that false ministers have a lack of respect, reverence and honor for the authority of local churches; and they especially have contempt for God's appointed authority — the pastor.

Peter uses the strong word "despise" to let us know how great their contempt for authority can become. They disdain, ridicule, condescend, tear down and deliberately try to make pastors look bad.

Why would they do this? By putting another down, they attempt to lift themselves up in the eyes of others.

Reckless and Arrogant

You may ask, "How in the world can they act like this inside the Church and get away with it? Why do people support this kind of abuse?"

Peter gives us the answer. He continues to say, "Presumptuous are they, self-willed, they are not afraid to speak evil of dignities."

The word "presumptuous" is from the Greek word *tolmetes* (tol-me-tes). It describes the attitude of a person who is "daring, brazen, determined, outspoken, candid" or "forward." This unbridled, negative and reckless behavior is confused by many to be boldness.

God's people have longed for strong spiritual leaders. Therefore, when a man stands in the pulpit and makes outrageously "daring, brazen, headstrong, shameless" and "reckless" statements — and does it in connection with scripture or under the guise of the anointing — *it somehow becomes acceptable.*

Like the example I gave at the first of this chapter, some will mistake this arrogance for "boldness" and begin to think, "Wow! This man is powerful! Listen to the way that he moves in authority and tells it like it is."

The unfortunate part of this is, if a person sitting under this shameless type of ministry has even the smallest seed of spiritual rebellion residing somewhere in his or her heart, *this will bring it forth!* They will probably mistake this terrible, behavior as "boldness" and thus, seek to duplicate it in their own spiritual life.

Very often this becomes a license to the immature to be unkind and ugly in the name of "boldness." Unfortunately, this often results in pastors being lambasted by immature people in their congregations, who now think that they are spiritual experts and know more about the minstry and the realm of the spirit than he.

Peter continues to tell us that these misguided prophets and teachers are also *"self-willed."*

The phrase "self-willed" is from the Greek word *authades* (au-tha-des) and is actually the Greek word for "arrogance." It denotes a person who is "obstinate toward others, determined to go his own way, and is willing to do what he wants — *at any cost* — to himself or to anyone else."

Then Peter says, "they are not afraid to *speak evil of dignities.*"

Once again, he clearly tells us that these belligerent individuals love to attack, defame, disdain and humiliate those who are in authority, and accuse them of a lack of spirituality.

Carefully Handling the Word

This idea of going "out into the spirit realm" to obtain our understanding of the Bible, and the command to stop using the mind, *perfectly illustrates* the point of someone who has gone overboard spiritually.

Saying that the Bible was "written in spirit, not in Hebrew or Greek," may sound deep and somewhat mystical to some people — but it makes no spiritual sense at all.

First of all, it is true that Jesus said, "The words that I speak unto you, they are spirit, and they are life" (John 6:63). It is also true, however, that the Holy Spirit chose to record those "spirit words" in the Old and New Testament languages of Hebrew and Greek.

Remember, "All scripture is given by inspiration of God. . . ." The word "inspiration" means that the Word actually contains the Divine life of God within it. How then, could you ever study it too much or too deeply?

It was the Bereans who were commended for their intensive study of the scriptures. Acts 17:11 says, "These were more noble than those in Thessalonica, in that they received the word with all readiness of mind, and searched the scriptures daily, whether those things were so."

I am quite certain that some of these off-base, fringe ministries today would have accused the Bereans of being "carnal" and "out of touch with the Spirit" because they were so given over to the study of God's Word. They may have even accused the Bereans of being "Word-bound."

But according to the Bible, the Bereans were not carnal, but rather, they were "more noble" than others because they searched the scriptures. *This was an act of nobility!*

Secondly, if all believers took this well-known minister's advise to "go out into the spirit realm" to get their understanding of the Bible, we would have spiritual anarchy in the Church — with thousands, perhaps millions, of different interpretations of the Word.

This is precisely the situation that the apostles were facing in the early days of the Church. The false prophet and false teacher "dogs" were ripping the Word to pieces. They were altering it, changing it, adding their own special revelations to it, and undermining its authority in the life of the Church.

Thus the reason Jude said that this faith was "delivered" to us for safe-keeping. Our responsibility before God is to study this Word, understand it, fine-tune ourselves to it, and then "pass it along" to others.

It was for this cause that Jude told the saints "to

earnestly contend for the faith that was once delivered unto the saints."

The false prophet, false teacher "dogs" then, as again today, were trying to rip this God-inspired, God-breathed Word to pieces and were replacing it with revelations of their own.

Chapter Eight
A New Twist to an Old Message

When giving his farewell address to the Ephesian elders in Acts 20:28-31, Paul said, "For I know this, that after my departing shall grievous wolves enter in among you, not sparing the flock."

He continues, "Also of your own selves shall men arise, speaking perverse things, to draw away disciples from them. Watch and remember, that by the space of three years I have not ceased to warn every one of you night and day with tears."

After all of Paul's warnings to them over a period of three full years, his prophetic utterance still came to pass! "Grievous wolves," similar to the mad "dogs" mentioned in Philippians 3:2, entered among the flock and began to "speak perverse things."

It is important to note the word "perverse." The word "perverse" is from the Greek word *diastrepho* (dia-stre-pho), which describes the act of "twisting, distorting" or "bending."

By using the word *diastrepho*, Paul makes his point very clear: false prophets and false teachers don't come with a brand new message, but rather, a "perversion" or "distortion" of the old.

A Teaching of a Different Kind

In order to combat this false prophet, false teacher problem head on, Paul left Timothy in Ephesus to deal with these doctrinal troublemakers. First Timothy 1:3 reads, "As I besought thee to abide still at Ephesus. . . that thou mightest charge some that they teach no *other doctrine.*"

The phrase "other doctrine" is taken from the Greek word *heterodidaskalos* (he-ter-o-di-das-ka-los), and is further evidence that the teaching Paul had previously entrusted to the Ephesian elders was now being distorted, twisted and perverted.

The phrase "other doctrine" (*heterodidaskalos*) is a compound of the words *heteros* and *didaskalos.* The word *heteros* refers to something that is "another of a different kind." It is where we get the word for a heterosexual, which is literally "a sex of a different kind."

The second part of the word, *didaskalos,* is simply the Greek word for "teaching." When compounded together, the word *heterodidaskalos* means a "teaching of a different kind," or a "teaching of a different nature."

Therefore, because Paul uses this word, he tells us that false prophets and false teachers may attempt to disguise their error to look like teaching, but in reality, they teach a "teaching of a different kind."

Their teaching may contain enough basic truth to make their message plausible, but in time, a false prophet or false teacher will start adding his or her own new revelations to that basically true message.

When it is all said and done, the basically true message that the fraudulent minister started out with is gone — and a new distorted, twisted and perverted message is left behind. So Paul says they teach a "teaching of a different kind."

Departing from the Faith in Galatia

Paul's letter to the Galatians clearly reveals that error-ridden ministries had made an advance upon the region of Galatia too. These fraudulent ministers were popping up all over!

In Galatians 1:6, Paul said, "I marvel that ye are so soon removed from him that called you into the grace of Christ unto another gospel. . . ."

Notice Paul says that they had been "removed" from the grace of Christ unto "another" gospel. The word "removed" and "another" are very important words in this verse.

The word "removed" is from the Greek word *metatithesthe* (me-ta-ti-thes-the) and it is a compound of two words, *meta* and *tithimi.* The word *meta* denotes a "change," and the word *tithimi* describes a "position." When taken together as one complete word, the word *metatithesthe* ("removed") denotes some kind of "positional change."

In other places where this word is translated correctly, it means "to transfer, remove, depart" or "to change one's opinion" about something. This word was also used in a military sense to describe rebellion against authority, insubordination, revolt or defection.

It is obvious from the usage of this word, that the error being taught in Galatia had caused quite a disturbance in the Church. Sweeping doctrinal changes were blowing through the Church — and like strong winds often do, they were making havoc of the house of God.

These strange new revelations were causing rebellion against leadership, insubordination, revolt and defection inside the Church.

Bewitched by a Magic Spell

From Paul's own words in Galatians 3:1, we know that seducing spirits had infiltrated the church in Galatia. In this verse, Paul says, "O, foolish Galatians, who hath bewitched you. . . ."

Notice, first of all, that Paul calls them "O, foolish Galatians." The word "foolish" is the Greek word *anoetos* (a-no-e-tos) and it describes "a person who acts without thinking, reasoning" or "using his or her mind."

This word indicates that the problem *isn't* that this person doesn't have a mind, but that he or she *refuses* to use their mind. This is a person who is mentally impotent by choice. He or she has refused to use their mind in a logical way.

It appears that a false sense of spirituality was in operation in the Galatian church. This false sense of spirituality *wrongly* told them that using their mind was carnal and unspiritual.

Fraudulent ministries will always tell you to "get out of your natural man," "Don't question what you see," "Don't try to understand the mysteries which we are giving you," "These supernatural manifestations are beyond your understanding," "Your mind is trying to rob you of supernatural possibilities. . . ."

God gave you your brain and did not intend for your spirit and mind to be in conflict with each other. Before you were saved, it is true that your mind was "enmity with God." However, now that you are regenerated by the Spirit of God, there is no reason that your mind and your spirit cannot cooperate together. This is God's best!

However, if a fraudulent minister can convince a crowd to shelve their minds, then he can easily coax them into believing almost anything. People who refuse to use their minds are the easiest people to "trick" and to "bewitch."

Paul asked the Galatians, "Who hath bewitched you. . . ." The word "bewitched" is taken from the Greek word *baskaino* (bas-kai-no) and literally means "to cast a spell on someone."

Paul's strong language tells us that this church had come under some type of demonic spell and the church, as a whole, had entered into the world of spiritual foolishness. This foolishness inside the Galatian church had grown so fast, that back in Galatians 1:6, he says, "I marvel that ye are so soon removed. . . ."

The word "marvel" is from the word *thaumadzo* (thau-mad-zo). It refers to "wonder, astonishment" or "amazement" about something. Paul was "astonished and amazed" that such ludicrous and absurd spiritual error had gotten a stronghold in this particular church.

Likewise, he is equally "astonished and amazed" that this seduction could happen so quickly. Thus, he says, "I marvel that ye are *so soon removed*. . . ." Then he identifies the type of teaching that was penetrating the church. He called it "another gospel."

The word "another" is again the Greek word *heteros*. This is the very word used in First Timothy 1:3, when Paul commanded Timothy to "charge some that they teach no *other doctrine*."

Because of Paul's frequent usage of this word at various and critical points in his epistles, no one can question the meaning of it. Just as they had done in Ephesus, false prophets and false teachers had invaded Galatia with a gospel of a "different kind."

To make his point even clearer, he continues in verse 7 by saying, "which is not another; but there be some that would trouble you, and would pervert the gospel of Christ."

Notice at the first of this verse, he says, " . . .which is not another. . . ." Now we have a very significant word change. This word for "another" is not the word *heteros*, but rather the Greek word *allos*, which refers to "something of the same kind."

To paraphrase this, Paul says, " . . .the gospel they preach is not like the gospel that we preach. . . it is not a gospel like ours at all."

Troublemakers!

He describes these false ministers as those "that would trouble you. . . ."

The word "trouble" is the word *tarasso* (ta-ras-so) and it refers to a "mental shaking up." It indicates that a shaking, tossing, anxious, excited, disturbance had occurred in the church.

These false prophets and false teachers may have even measured their spiritual power by how much they had shaken the people up with their ministries. I can almost hear them saying, *"Boy, we really shook 'em up tonight!"* *"Yeah! We had that place rock'in and let 'em have it!"* *"Whew — they never knew what hit them!"*

However, what they call "boldness," the apostle Paul calls "trouble." These crafty, underhanded, cunning opportunists had made a royal mess of the gospel Paul had preached to the church in Galatia. They took the simple doctrine of grace and multilated it with all of their new additions! These troublemakers were making wreckage of the church.

According to Paul, they "perverted the gospel of Christ." The word "pervert" used in this verse, is the word *metastrepho* (me-ta-stre-pho), which means "to reverse, turn aside, turn about, bend" or "change."

This is what they were doing with the gospel! They were taking the simple message of the cross and were adding so many new revelations to it, that the simplistic message of the gospel was now "bent, changed, twisted" and almost "reversed."

Spiritual Perversion

Almost the same identical, ridiculous spiritual error was being duplicated in the church at Ephesus.

When Timothy arrived in Ephesus to set things in order, what a mess he found on his hands! He discovered that his leadership in Ephesus was infected with a spiritual sickness, which later in time came to be known as *Gnosticism*.

It is highly possible that some of these same infected leaders who were now causing problems had been there when Paul lovingly bid the elders farewell in Acts 20:28-31. It was to this very group of men that Paul said, "Of your own selves shall men arise, speaking perverse things, to draw away disciples from them."

Just as Paul had previously warned them, slowly and seductively, spiritual perversion began to work its way into the mainstream of the church.

Gnosticism: Spiritual Arrogance in Disguise

The name "Gnosticism" is taken from the Greek word *gnosis* (gno-sis), and it means "knowledge." It's most often-used form in the New Testament is the word *ginosko* (gi-no-sko), which simply means, "I know."

However, as time went by the word *gnosis* came to carry a more definitive meaning. Soon it was used to describe individuals or groups who believed they had special, superior revelations that were better and higher than any one else's.

These so-called possessors of "special knowledge" boasted of having been beyond the veil of the spirit, seeing what no other eye had ever seen, hearing what no other ear had ever heard, and going boldly where no man had ever gone before.

With this new revelation in hand, they began to invade the church with their exaggerated revelations, thus luring "disciples after them."

With their outlandish claims of new visions, dreams, revelations, fresh insights never before recorded in scripture, and other genuinely odd supernatural phenomena, these "specially enlightened ones" began to draw huge crowds of thrilled listeners into a web of deception that eventually produced a mindless, idiotic, spiritual excess.

Learning the Tricks of the Trade

At this same time in history, there was a secular group of wandering lecturers who traveled and gave speeches as a vocation. These traveling speakers gained great acclaim for themselves. They were called " Sophists."

The term Sophist is a derivative of the Greek word *sophos* (so-phos). Technically, it means "wisdom." Just as the Gnostics claimed to have "special knowledge," the Sophists claimed to have "special wisdom."

These Sophists were the secular world's counterpart to the idiotic Gnostic teachers inside the church. In a very real way, their "wisdom" and teachings were just as idiotic as those of the Gnostics.

The Sophists were on the scene long before the Church of Jesus Christ. By examining the razzle-dazzle, flamboyant style of Sophists, it is emphatically clear that the Sophist's well-known, popular style influenced the Gnostic prophets and teachers, and contributed to the spiritual excess that eventually developed inside the church.

Because the Sophists were so immensely popular, as time went by, it appeared that many Christian leaders (notably the Gnostics) who were impressed with their style, took them as a *role model* for their traveling ministries.

Sophists traveled as a profession from city to city, very similar to the way that traveling ministries do today. This was their lifestyle. They gave lectures to giant crowds, who at times came from great distances to hear them speak. Some of these eloquent, smooth-talking orators had worked the circuit for so long, that they were listed among the greatest celebrities of the day and were even household names. This was "Hollywood" of the ancient world.

To ensure a large turnout at their meetings, they would study the community where they were going to give their speech, and after research, they would determine what was the most controversial and emotional issue in the city.

After selecting that emotion-packed subject as the topic of their speech, they sent their workers out into the streets to invite the general public to come and hear them. They changed their message from city to city and group to group.

You might say they were the original "ear ticklers."

Because there were so many Sophists traveling and striving for a place of notoriety, they were intensely competitive with one another. There was *no limit* to the flamboyance they would use to grab the ear of the people.

Sensationalism and controversy was the name of the game for Sophists — and they knew how to play that game very well.

Led by the Shouts of the Crowd

Ordinarily, the content of their messages made little sense. Substance and truthfulness in their speeches were a very low, low priority.

Their chief concern was to provide a spectacular, earth-shaking, sensational afternoon of controversy that would get the people back to the next lecture. They were so morally irresponsible, that they were frequently known to speak for hours on end about subjects they knew nothing about, pretending to be experts on the subject.

They were con-artists of the highest order, and simply knew how to "sound wiser" than anyone else. It would be very accurate to label them as unethical, untruthful, unfair, dishonorable, immoral, unscrupulous and totally unreliable.

One historian has said, "they were like men walking in darkness — led only by the shouts of the crowd and the clapping and applause of the masses."

Setting the Pattern for Sensationalism

It was after the pattern of the Sophists, that the Gnostic prophets and teachers *patterned* their ministries. For this cause, sensationalism was the main theme to a Gnostic prophet or teacher's message.

It was very easy to discern whether or not a minister was a Gnostic. Gnostics did not preach the Word with the same strong emphasis that had characterized the preaching and teaching of the apostles.

Gnostics specialized in supernatural phenomena, such as visits with angels, trips to heaven and beyond, and even time-travel to places in the past. This is what most Gnostic teachings were concerned with.

There was, of course, those Gnostics who had pure hearts and believed they were genuinely on the cutting edge of a new move of God. The Montanists, a Gnostic group from around the year A.D. 170, clearly loved the Lord. They undoubtedly, at least at first, moved in genuine manifestations of the Holy Spirit.

In time, however, even this group who seemed to start out on the right track, was perverted by unfounded teachings and phenomena that had no basis or root in scripture. Like other Gnostic groups before and after them, it all became sensationalism for the sake of attracting and holding a crowd's attention.

As long as the crowd was pleased, entertained and excited to come back to the next meeting, the Gnostics felt they had done a good job. Who knows, they may have judged the strength of the anointing by the response of the people.

To some degree this same spiritual environment is trying to recreate itself in the church again and a brand new breed of Gnostics are appearing on the scene with inordinate claims of new revelation.

Mesmerizing and Tantalizing Tales

To simply teach the Word would have been out of the question for these super-spiritual Gnostic revelators.

In their view of things, the Bible was just foundational; a "starting point." You couldn't stay "on the milk" forever. Their behavior and messages asserted that mature spiritual people went beyond the teaching of Word, and out into the realm of the spirit to receive new spiritual enlightenment.

Lengthy conversations with angels, demonic apparitions, trips to heaven, visits with other never-before-known celestial beings, as I said before, were the source of most of their teachings. Oh yes, there was some truth mingled together with their message; just enough to make their message acceptable.

Their stories were so mesmerizing and tantalizing, that people moved to the edge of their seats in anticipation of hearing their next incredible, absolutely stupendous statement.

Though totally unsubstantiated by scripture, their teachings and utterances were captivating, fascinating and interesting. Even by today's standards, a Gnostic teaching would be very entertaining and enjoyable.

One Gnostic even purported that he was transported back in time to Bethlehem, so he could watch Jesus Christ be born! Why did he say this was necessary? In order that he might fill in all the details surrounding Jesus Christ's birth, that the gospels' writers had supposedly not written.

It is hard to believe the church would have ever gotten involved with something so ridiculous and out of line with scripture.

Yet, it is obvious that this problem is not really that far removed from us today. The woman with oil and blood appeared to have no problem convincing a large crowd of people that she had the real feathers of the Holy Spirit in her meeting!

The Purpose of Dreams, Visions and Revelations

Rather than face life head-on and deal with changes that desperately need to be made in their lives, many believers sidestep reality and turn toward the supernatural in hope of an instant solution. If not a permanent cure, then they desire to obtain temporary relief from reality.

This is why the Gnostics were so popular in Paul's day, and why false ministers are still so popular today. They provide "a way out" — it is a form of *spiritual escapism*. Because it is wrapped in the guise of a deeper spirituality, it is much more difficult to identify and correct.

This, of course, is not true of everyone. Many of my own dearest friends move mightily in the gifts of the Holy Spirit, and are frequented by dreams, visions and supernatural visitations. These gifts are a part of my own ministry. If, for some reason, we are not personally familiar with these, then we *should* be. This is the supernatural heritage of the Church.

When the official record of Christianity is closed and finished at the coming of Jesus Christ, I want that record to reflect that Rick Renner was completely convinced on the basis of scripture, that dreams, visions and prophetic utterances are valid experiences for the Church today, and are in fact, evidence of the Spirit's outpouring in the last days.

Joel 2:28 says, "And it shall come to pass afterward, I will pour my Spirit upon all flesh; and your sons and your daughters shall prophesy, your old men shall dream dreams, your young men shall see visions."

The statistics show that *one third* of the Book of Acts deals with supernatural activity, and *one tenth* of the Book of Acts tells of people who received personal direction for their lives through some supernatural means. This being the case, we should not be surprised when a fellow believer encounters a supernatural experience.

In the Book of Acts, we are told that "cloven tongues of fire" appeared in the upper room (Acts 2); people were healed by Peter's shadow (Acts 5); Philip was supernaturally transported by the Spirit to Gaza (Acts 8); an angel rescued Peter from danger (Acts 12); a supernatural earthquake was sent to set Paul and Silas free from prison (Acts 16); and the anointing was transmitted to the sick and afflicted through pieces of cloth (Acts 19).

This Book of Acts was meant to be a *pattern book*, not just a history book. If this is so, then one third of our Christian life should be comprised of supernatural experiences, and one tenth of all the personal direction we receive should come from supernatural sources.

My own call to the ministry came to me during a vision in 1974. In 1985, I had a vision of Jesus, during which the Lord instructed me concerning my ministry. Once again, in 1987, the Lord appeared to me in a vision and instructed me concerning the direction of my ministry.

I thank God for each of these experiences. However, these experiences were not given to me so that I could teach them as a new doctrine. These were given for personal direction for my life and ministry. If I used these experiences to elevate my own spirituality in the eyes of others, and make them the "mecca" that others should aspire unto, I would be *grossly wrong*.

God sends these into our lives for the sake of confirmation of scripture and personal direction. To tell others that they must have the same encounter I have had, is like putting them in a new form of legalism. To be spiritual, their experiences would have to match mine.

Rather than forcing others to follow in your steps of spirituality, allow God to reveal Himself to them in His own way. Yes, it is good to share your experiences. It encourages others to open their hearts to God.

But be careful that you do not elevate yourself or your experience so highly, that others are intimidated and feel spiritually inferior because they haven't had the same experience. Let God be God. He wants to reveal Himself to every man and woman in His own wonderful way.

Spiritual Hallucinators

But there are those people who use dreams and visions as a way to hide from the pressures of life.

A real visitation from God will equip you and assist you to face your challenge with new courage and a new confidence that God is going to move on your behalf. Rather than hide from life, you'll be ready to "take on the world!"

Spiritual hallucinators are those people who are looking for some super-duper spiritual experience to "take them away from the world." They want an experience that will get them out of the kitchen, away from a soured marriage, far from dirty diapers, a negative check balance, and so on.

These people are seeking a *hallucination,* not a *visitation.* A visitation would equip them to live victoriously in the middle of a filthy kitchen, dirty diapers, a soured marriage, and financial difficulties. A hallucination, on the other hand, is nothing more than *a spiritualized form of irresponsibility and running from reality.*

Nearly every pastor has had to deal with individuals whose lives are out of order, who have a marriage on the rocks, cannot keep a job for more than a month at a time, and yet, this person believes God has called them into a worldwide ministry!

I have met scores of men who believe God has called them to bless the kingdom of God financially. They have told me, "Brother Rick, God has called me to be a giver. He is going to bless me with millions so I can give into your ministry and others, too."

Yet, when I ask the pastor about the man, he tells me, "Oh, don't pay any attention to him. He hasn't been able to keep a job for two years, and he is the most financially irresponsible person in the church."

These types of individuals use dreams and visions as a form of escapism and a cover-up for their personal indiscretions. This, my friend, is a hallucination, not a visitation!

These types of hallucinations don't change your life; they just delay dealing with the problems until a later time.

Noah and Norea

Thanks to an archeological discovery in Egypt, near the city of Nag Hammadi, in the year 1945, some of the fantastically strange teachings of the Gnostics are still with us today.

Though the particular writings that were discovered at Nag Hammadi are dated later than the New Testament (circa. A.D. 350), these are a perfect reflection of what the Gnostic prophets and teachers began to teach in the church.

The following is a literal story from one of the Gnostic scriptures from those early days. This was their *new revelation* about Noah and his wife, Norea!

In the name of Spirit-inspired revelation, they claimed that the Holy Spirit had supernaturally revealed to them the name of Noah's wife. According to them, her name was Norea.

The Bible never once tells us what was the name of Noah's wife. Therefore, this was a typical Gnostic revelation. *It went beyond the written Word and filled in all the blank spaces.*

But wait! There is more. . . .

Lo and behold, they received another revelation. "Norea was the seventh daughter of Adam and Eve." This, of course, can neither be proven nor substantiated by scripture. However, it does make for a very interesting story!

Finally, after a period of time, a whole new story about Noah and his wife, Norea, emerged.

Once the Ark was built, the Gnostics reported, Noah saw this was his perfect opportunity to finally get rid of Norea. Why would Noah do this? Though there is no scripture for it, the Gnostics taught that Noah and Norea had a volatile marriage.

According to their "revelation," when Noah entered the Ark, he hastily shut the door behind him so Norea could not get inside. By shutting her out of the huge ship, he hoped that Norea would be caught in the raging current of the flood and be forever swept away.

Infuriated by her husband's actions, the Gnostics claimed that Norea blew against the Ark with her breath, and burned it down to the ground.

So Noah, they said, built a second ship. While she was preparing to burn her husband's ship for the second time, she was abruptly interrupted when evil looking creatures, called archons, surrounded her. According to the Gnostics, archons were demonic creatures who ruled the world.

They said to Norea, "Give us what your mother gave us!" "What did my mother give you?" Norea asked. "Your mother, Eve, gave us sexual relations! Render us service. . . now!"

Norea answered them, "You did not know my mother. . . it was someone else that you knew!" Just then, the archons turned black with anger and violently demanded, "Render us service!"

In this panic-stricken moment, Norea fell to the ground on her face and began to scream out for help from heaven. Suddenly and unexpectedly, a huge angel in bright raiment descended out of the spirit realm in response to her screams.

Upon seeing the giant angel, the archons withdrew their attack on Norea and retreated back into the dark corridors of the nether world.

Norea looked at the giant, angelic creature and asked, "Who are you?" He answered, "I am Eleleth, the great angel that stands in the presence of the Holy Spirit, and I am come to save you from these lawless spirits. . . ."

Believe it or not, this is just *the beginning* of the story.

Entertaining, but Irrelevant

This is just one example of the Gnostic teaching that was beginning to pervade the church. They also wrote theological books that contained new ideas about God, a God-mother, creation, angels, Lucifer as the brother of Jesus, new facts to be added to both Old and New Testament stories, and so on.

For a mere sampling of how far "off" and out-of-balance

a person can become, here is a brief list of books from the First, Second, and Third Centuries that contained their new, spectacular revelations.

Some are these are: "The Archontics," "The Octect of Subsistent Entities," "The Elect Transcend the World," "The Book of Thomas," "The Egyptian Gospel," "The Foreigner," "The Gospel According to Philip," "The Gospel of Truth," "The Secret Book According to John," "The Hymn of the Pearl," "The Reality of the Evil Rulers," "Adam's Faculty of Speech," "Jesus' Digestive System," "The Hypostasis of the Archons," "The Origin of the World," "The Three Tales of Seth," "The Thought of Norea" and "The Sacred Book of the Great Invisible Spirit."

It is right to ask, "How could anyone get so extremely far off?" "How could anyone be seduced into such ridiculous, vain speculation and error?"

The Entrance of Grievous Wolves

The apostle Paul had plainly said, "For I know this, that after my departure shall grievous wolves enter in among you, not sparing the flock. Also of your own selves shall men arise, speaking perverse things, to draw away disciples after them" (Acts 20:29-30).

Prior to the First Century, while Paul and the other apostles were still ministering, writing New Testament scriptures and establishing churches, this Gnostic problem, though it was rapidly growing and was dangerous to the faith, was a controllable one.

Because the apostles knew of the foreboding dangers of this Gnostic influence, they counteracted this error with the strong, strong teaching of scripture and apostolic doctrine.

However, after the death of the last apostle (John), and toward the middle of the First Century, there was a noted change in what was being preached by the leadership of the Church.

In fact, this change was so dramatic that by the year A.D. 170, the seeds of Gnosticism had started to come full-bloom in many places. Things were getting so profoundly out of balance that the Montanists, covered earlier in this chapter, began to gain widespread popularity.

Though they appeared to have started out as a genuine move of God's Spirit, in time their teachings became accompanied by extremely strange behavior, such as prophetic utterances that sounded like the "barking" of dogs. All of this, they claimed, was the beginning of a new move of the Spirit of God.

Then around the year A.D. 200, things began to change *fast* and *dramatically*. In addition to these serious doctrinal problems that were emerging, the power and gifts of the Holy Spirit began to wane in the church.

From the writings of early church Fathers such as Hippolytus, Novatian, Tertullian, Cyprian, Origen and Firmilian, we know that the gifts of the Spirit were definitely in operation at this time; however, they were not in operation like they had been before.

Very slowly, the gifts of the Holy Spirit were beginning to vanish. Finally, there was only a trace of the Spirit's supernatural presence in the Church, and by the year A.D. 260, the gifts of the Holy Spirit had vanished from the Church altogether. They were gone.

What Happened to the Life of the Spirit?

Did these spiritual manifestations "pass away" with the death of the last apostle, as many denominational churches allege? Positively not!

An overview of historical dates proves that the gifts of the Holy Spirit were in some kind of manifestation for nearly 160 years after John, the last of the original apostles, died.

Then what happened to the life of the Spirit? Where did it go?

During the First Century, when the original apostles were alive and ministering, there was a heavy emphasis on *apostolic teaching* — which eventually became *the New Testament scriptures*. At this time, there was an abundance of signs, wonders, miracles and divers gifts of the Holy Spirit.

Then toward the end of the First Century, and into the middle of the Second Century, when the apostles were gone, Paul's prediction began to be fulfilled. "Grievous wolves" entered in among the flock.

This is when these strange forms of Gnosticism began to take hold of the Church. With the strong leadership of the apostles out of the way, these fraudulent ministers with ulterior motives began to make in-roads into the Church at an alarming rate of speed.

Respect for the Word of God had deteriorated to such an extent, that the faithful bishop Polycarp, known as "the great teacher of Asia," in regard to Paul's writings, said: "I am persuaded that ye are well-trained in the sacred writings, and nothing is hidden from you. But to myself this is not granted."

In other words, this well-known bishop who was called "the great teacher of Asia," was for all practical purposes unfamiliar with Paul's writings by his own admission!

The spiritual atmosphere of the Church began to rapidly decline as people moved away from the teaching of the apostles toward other so-called "deeper things". Over a period of time, the foundational teachings of the apostles were nearly discarded, and an abnormal emphasis to receive brand new revelation came into a place of prominence.

Remove the Word, Remove the Power

At first, this departure from the Word took place very slowly. Thus, there was still enough Word being preached at the beginning of the First Century for the Holy Spirit to confirm with signs and wonders.

But eventually, this drifting away from the Word became so gross, so far removed from the message the apostles preached, so far off into strange and curious teachings, that there was no longer enough Word being preached for the Holy Spirit to confirm.

Church history reveals that the strong teachings of the apostles had almost been entirely replaced. Gnostic messages, ecclesiastical structures, orthodoxy unrelated to scripture and apostolic pattern, legalism and other such things, had usurped the place of the Word.

It wasn't long after these changes began to be accepted and practiced (circa. A.D. 260), that the gifts and power of the Holy Spirit ceased to function in the Church.

The strong presence of the Spirit was attached to the strong teaching of the Word. When the Word was gone, the Spirit's power was gone too.

This departing from "the faith" in pursuit of greater spiritual experiences eventually robbed them of the very thing that they were seeking: *God's power.*

With the teaching of the Word gone, the power and gifts of the Holy Spirit disappeared and spiritual darkness began to fill the Church. Soon after this, the world was ushered into that horribly dark chapter in history which we call "The Dark Ages."

From time to time after this, there would be occasional revivals of supernatural power. Every time this occurred, it happened during a period when the Word of God was being re-emphasized. This brought the gifts and power of the Spirit back into the church.

Therefore, if we want power, we must learn a lesson from history and stick to the Word. *These two — the Word and power — are inseparable.*

Chapter Nine
Thievish, Pillaging and Plundering Predators

With tantalizing and mesmerizing tales in hand, false prophets and false teachers stepped forward and began to lure the early Church away from the foundational teaching of God's Word that had "once for all been delivered unto the saints."

Ingenious, polished and professional, these pseudo prophets and phony teachers were masters at manipulating people with extravagant stories. With incredible skill, they enticed and whetted the appetite of the spiritually hungry, thus causing their mouths to water for higher and deeper experiences.

By taking advantage of their God-given hunger for spiritual reality, they baited the saints with their sensational tales of unfounded trips to heaven, newfangled ideas about angels and fresh disclosures about Noah and Norea, and the Doctrine of the Laughing Saviour (just to mention a few of these tales).

By dangling such stories in front of the spiritually hungry and enticing them with their extravagant tales, they were able to persuade well-meaning and sincere believers to jump off the edge of reality into an unwholesome obsession for weird experiences which had no root or foundation in the Word of God.

Rather than equipping the saints to live successfully for

Jesus Christ as solid, responsible Christian witnesses, these counterfeit ministers purposed to make their listeners utterly dependant upon themselves.

Their intention was clearly to "hook" the saints and make them spiritually addicted to their own ministries. Paul's own words echo to us once again: "of your own selves shall men arise, speaking perverse things, to draw away disciples after them" (Acts 20:30).

With this purpose of "drawing away discples after them" in mind, very slowly and methodically they began to set traps of deception that would snare the saints and induce them into the bondage of spiritual slavery.

Spiritual Hostages

This is precisely why Paul wrote to the Colossian church and sternly told them, "Beware lest any man spoil you through philosophy and vain deceit" (Colossians 2:8).

When Paul begins this plea to the Colossian church, notice that he begins by using the word "beware." He minces no words when he writes to them about the deception that was worming its way into their midst. Right from the start of this pleading verse, he hits them hard and strong and tells them to be on their guard. The word "beware" is from the Greek word *blepete* (ble-pe-te) and means "watch out, be on your guard" or "look!"

The fact that Paul would use such "alarmist" language, assuredly tells us that impending danger was all around the Colossian church. It was imminent.

False prophets and false teachers were making inroads to this church at an alarming rate of speed. In fact, spiritual perversion here had become so bad that they had actually begun *the practice of worshipping angels!*

This was the reason Paul began his warning to them in such strong terms. He wanted to alert them to the *spiritually hazardous condition* that was growing in their midst.

Thievish, Pillaging and Plundering Predators

Because this outrageous activity was beginning to "spoil" the church, Paul told them, "Let no man spoil you. . . ."

The word "spoil" is from the Greek word *sulogogeo* (su-lo-go-geo). It was a technical word used to describe the violent behavior of a hostile army who invaded an innocent and unsuspecting land. Today we would call this a brutal attack upon humanity.

What a word for Paul to use! *This is a vivid description of kidnapping, bloodshed, rape and plunder!*

Invading armies, like the one Paul is using in this verse, had a horrible reputation for raping women, killing children, burning down homes, robbing people of their personal possessions and destroying everything in their path as they marched along.

The greatest tragedy that accompanied this type of invasion, was when the enemy took over a new geographical area, they immediately pounced upon familes and broke them up — and they took special delight in capturing the younger family members to be their own personal slaves in foreign countries.

Such strong language tells us that Paul is trying to slap the saints awake — out of a spiritual stupor — to realize evil was lurking in their midst. If they did not deal with this problem bravely, soon the church would be utterly ravaged.

Because Paul uses this word "spoil" in his warning to the Colossians, like Jude did in his epistle, he is painting *a graphic picture of warfare* in the mist of the Colossian church.

The church of Colosse — a truly innocent and genuinely spiritually hungry church — was in critical danger of being exploited, abused and scandalized by false prophets and false teachers who wanted to pillage and plunder the saints for their own personal gain.

If their attack inside the church turned out as they planned, the Colossian church would end up like a divided, deeply wounded family, and would be torn to pieces by ambition, disagreement and discord.

If the fraudulent minister's plans worked extremely well, these pseudo ministers would make it appear that the leadership of the church was at fault for all the problems.

With such confusion in the ranks, it would then be easy for them to move in, pick up the pieces, and draw these believers after themselves.

An Appeal that was Hard to Resist

Like experienced strategists who meticulously plan every step of their attack, these lying ministers used a bait and worked a strategy which they knew the saints could *not resist!*

Paul says, "Beware lest any man spoil you through philosophy and vain deceit."

The word "philosophy" is taken from the Greek word *philosophia* (phi-lo-so-phia). It is a compound of the words *philos* (phi-los) and *sophia* (so-phia).

Philos is one of many words for "love," and *sophia* is the Greek word for "wisdom." The word *sophia* is the same word from which the Sophists (covered in Chapter 8) derived their name. When these two words, *philos* and *sophia*, are compounded together, they form the word *philosophia*, which literally means "a love of wisdom."

This is exactly the appeal that the false prophets and false teachers were using to seduce the church. They were baiting the saints with new revelations that sounded deep, profound and mystical. From all outward appearances, it seemed that these preachers possessed "special wisdom."

By tempting the spiritually sincere with their so-called "wisdom," they drew the saints into their well-planned, strategized web of deception.

If they tried to entice the saints with blatant, outright lies, their attempts would have been futile. *This would have been too obvious.* Therefore, they tempted them with something that sounded good; something that was close to the truth; and something that was highly revered: *wisdom.*

Just as the serpent tempted Eve with the fruit of the tree, they were showing off their new revelations and were telling the saints that these new teachings were required to "make one wise" (Genesis 3:6).

Pointless Delusions and Nightmares

Paul continues to say, "Beware lest any man spoil you through philosophy and *vain deceit....*"

It is as though Paul says, "Let me tell you the truth about these super-spirituals who claim to possess special light and wisdom. In reality, their new revelations are nothing more than a lot of wasted talk. It is a lot of *vain deceit."*

The phrase "vain deceit" gives us Paul's very strong opinion about the kind of teachings that the false ministers were using to attract the attention of the Colossian church.

The word "vain" is from the Greek word *kenos* (ke-nos) and it is used 18 times throughout the New Testament. It always stands for something that is "empty, hollow" or "wasted."

The word "deceit" is from the Greek word *apate* (a-pa-te) and it refers to a "delusion" or a "hallucination." *A delusion is a fantasy, an aberation, or a nightmare.*

What you discover is what the false prophets and false teachers have labeled "wisdom," the apostle Paul calls "empty, hollow, wasted delusions and nightmares!"

These make-believe prophets and phony teachers were nothing more than hallucinators who were dreaming up stories and feeding delusions to the church at large in the name of new, God-given revelation.

If this falsehood was not corrected soon, it would truly create *a nightmarish situation!* By buying the lies that these sinister ministers were feeding them, they would soon be infected by this spiritual sickness and drawn away as "spoil" for these fraudulent leaders.

Therefore, Paul tells them in no uncertain terms, "Let no man spoil you through philosophy and vain deceit. . . ."

Disqualified from Service

Along this same line of thought, in Colossians 2:18, Paul states, "Let no man beguile you of your reward in a voluntary humility and worshipping of angels, intruding into those things which he hath not seen, vainly puffed up by his fleshly mind."

Five important points are covered in this verse. The first point is found in the word "beguile," the second is found in the word "voluntary," the third in the word "humility," the fourth is taken from the word "intruding," and the last point, the fifth one, is from the phrase "vainly puffed up."

First, we must look at the word "beguile." The word "beguile" is from the Greek word *katabrabeuo* (ka-ta-bra-beu-o) and it is a compound of the Greek words *kata* and *brabeuo.*

Kata nearly always describes a downward action, and can be translated as "down" or "against." The second part of the word, *brabeuo,* was a technical word to picture an "umpire" or "judge" of the atheletic games.

When the two words are compounded together into one word, thus forming the word *katabrabeuo,* they depict an umpire or judge of the athletic games, who has just eliminated an athelete from participating in any future events.

This word indicates that dishonorable behavior has been committed by the athlete. In view of these facts that have been presented to the judge, the judge has found a serious "strike against him." Therefore, the judge has eliminated him — from competing in the games. *He has been disqualified.*

Don't Succumb to Pressure from Others

By using this word in the context of this verse, Paul tells

us that deceived leaders will try to pressure others into following their same spiritual error.

If the deceived leader comes across another leader who sees things a little differently from him and takes a different spiritual approach, the deceived leader, threatened by this, may try to use his or her influence with others to discredit that person.

In other words, he may try to eliminate and disqualify you from public ministry in order to get you out of the way. Your solid stand on your own convictions, and your refusal to "go with the crowd," represents a strong threat to this type of individual. Therefore, this false leader may tell others that you are unspiritual, carnal and out-of-touch with what the Spirit of God is currently doing.

Perhaps he will even claim that you are a part of the "old move" of God and that you are not willing to make the adjustments necessary to be included in the next move of God.

You must know that deceived leaders detest those whom they cannot influence or sway. If you are immovable in your stand on God's Word, then this person may simply try to *eliminate* you and *disqualify* you in the eyes of others.

Regardless of how much pressure these fraudulent gifts place on you to conform to their ways, the Word of God demands that you resist their pressure and stand strong to your own Biblically-based convictions.

Forcing Supernatural Experiences

Then we come to the second important point in Colossians 2:18. Paul continues to say, "Let no man beguile you of your reward in *a voluntary humility. . . .*"

The word "voluntary" is taken from the Greek word *thelo* (the-lo). It literally means "I will," "I wish" or "I desire."

Since Paul uses the word *thelo* in this verse, we know

that the Colossian extremists were making their supernatural experiences happen as a result of their own sheer "will."

Honestly, it makes one wonder if these deceived leaders had ever experienced a real supernatural encounter with God. If they had, then they would have known that real visitations from God cannot be forced at "will."

Yet, this is exactly what the false prophets and false teachers of Paul's day were doing. In order to prove their spirituality to themselves and to others, they were attempting to force their way out into the realm of the spirit in order to obtain mystical experiences.

As you shall see in the pages to come, Paul insinuates that most of their supernatural phenomena didn't come from the spirit realm; but rather, came from their over-active imaginations!

An Outward Show of Humility

Also carefully observe the third important point that Paul makes. He continues, "Let no man beguile you of your reward through a voluntary *humility. . . .*"

In Greek, the word "humility" is the word *tapeinophrosune* (ta-pei-no-phro-su-ne), and it is a compound of the words *tapeinos* and *phrosune*. *Tapeinos* denotes the idea of "humbleness," and the word *phrosune* is the Greek word for the "intelligence" or "mind." When compounded, they carry the idea of "lowliness of mind." This is "a modest appraisal of one's self."

Why would Paul use this word of "modesty" to portray false prophets and false teachers?

Because false prophets and false teachers are smooth operators. Rather than announce their new revelations and teachings in a brazen and dogmatic way, these troublemakers have learned the power of a modest disguise. *This disguise of humility makes them much more dangerous to the church.*

Why?

No false prophet or false teacher is more dangerous than the one who walks in the pretense of humility; pretending to possess a reverence for the things of the Spirit; and walking in a false humility about his or her own spiritual experiences and adventures.

On account of the fact that the Body of Christ is sincere and pure at heart, when they see the appearance of sincerity in a leader, they view this leader as one whom they can trust.

Therefore, this outward show of false humility can impart a certain amount of credibility to false prophets and false teachers in the eyes of the people. Because they possess the "appearance" of humility about themselves and their experiences, people often open their hearts to them and to their strange revelations.

Intruders with Over-active Imaginations

However, Paul makes it emphatically clear that their experiences were false! In his fourth point, he tells us that a false prophet or false teacher is constantly *"intruding into those things which he hath not seen. . . ."*

What an insult this must have been to the fraudulent leaders who were reading Paul's epistle! They knew exactly who Paul was referring to in his letter: *themselves!*

Paul calls them "intruders." The word "intruding" is from the Greek word *embateuo* (em-ba-teu-o) and it literally means "to penetrate, examine, investigate, scrutinize" or "to search out." The foremost meaning of the word, however, is the idea of "penetration."

This is just *exactly* what the Gnostics were claiming to have accomplished. By their actions, their words, their teachings and behavior, they declared they had "penetrated" the knowledge barrier and had been beyond the veil of the flesh.

Paul shoots it straight when he describes these bogus prophets and teachers. He says they "intrude into those things which he hath not seen. . . ."

In other words, you could paraphrase Paul's words as

follows: "you didn't penetrate the spirit realm and have a genuine vision from God. You just have an imagination that works overtime."

Modern Day Trips to Heaven and Beyond

In light of this message from Paul about forced experiences, when you consider some of the visions of heaven that have been recorded in best-selling books in recent years, one cannot help but *wonder* if some of these are simply the work of an over-active imagination, rather than the Spirit of God.

For instance, when people come back from heaven with details about how their heavenly mansions are decorated; and when they come back telling about lengthy conversations which they have had with dead saints, who told them new details about the Word that are not recorded in scripture; then we have some very *questionable material* on our hands.

Such teaching has been very popular in recent years. It was popular and sensational during Paul's day too. There is no doubt in my mind, personally, that much of this type of teaching is a revival of Gnostic influence in the Church once again.

Though these kinds of teachings may be popular and entertaining and sell a lot of books, these kinds of facts and stories are usually unfounded and unsubstantiated by scripture.

Even if such stories were true, they cannot form the foundation for our belief or faith.

Besides this, while we cannot say that these types of stories violate what the Bible says about heaven — *since there surely must be much of heaven that is not recorded in scripture* — it is absolutely clear that the majority of these new tales of heaven are not in agreement with the examples of people who have been to heaven in scripture.

What do I mean by this?

When Biblical characters went to heaven and recorded

the events that they saw there, they did not come back talking about how their mansions were decorated. Neither can you find one scriptural account where they recorded that they had conversations with saints that had died and were waiting for them there.

On the contrary, people in scripture who were granted the privilege of seeing heaven were filled with awe and wonder "for Him that sitteth upon the throne." After seeing Jesus, high and lifted up, everything else in heaven faded in comparison to His majesty and beauty.

Thus, when you study the writings of the Old Testament writers, and even the New Testament accounts of heaven, you will find only statements and memories of worship, adoration and praise.

There is no mention of the decor of their mansions. Similarly, there is no mention of any conversation with dead saints. These are non-existent in scripture, and scripture is our foundation for belief and doctrine.

However, because there surely must be vast realities of heaven which never had been recorded, we cannot say that people have lied about their experiences. On other hand, we can say with great certainty that their lengthy stories do not appear to line up with the spirit of scripture.

When the apostle Paul recorded his own experience in heaven which followed his stoning between Lystra and Derbe (Acts 14:19-20), he said he heard "unspeakable words, which are not lawful for a man to utter" (Second Corinthians 12:4).

When I hear other ministries speak at great lengths about what they heard and saw in heaven, I cannot help but ponder on Paul's words. It makes me wonder, "Are these new ministers greater than Paul himself?"

Paul, who wrote the majority of the New Testament scriptures, was not permitted to share the things which he had seen and heard in heaven. Yet, there are scores of people today who claim to have all types of new insight into the details of heaven that are not recorded in scripture.

The problem *isn't* their claim that they have gone to heaven, or have seen heaven in a vision. Many people have been to heaven in scripture. I am thoroughly convinced that many people have been to heaven and back in our own day, by means of a vision or perhaps a near-death experience.

In addition to the questionable accounts of heaven that have been sold in recent years, many wonderful accounts of heavenly visits have been written that *do* agree with the Word of God, and can be substantiated by scripture.

Enoch was translated to heaven; Elijah had visions of heaven; Stephen saw the Lord in heaven as he was stoned to death; Paul had gone into the third heaven after his stoning between Lystra and Derbe; and the apostle John had the most spectacular view of heaven that any man has ever had.

However, when we begin to add details to heaven that are not even recorded in the Word of God, we are on *shaky ground.* Why would God reveal more now to someone else, than He has already recorded in His Word?

This is indeed a Gnostic problem. If the apostle Paul were still alive and with us today, he would deal quite boldly with this kind of teaching. He would probably call it "vain deceit." In other words, he would call it "an empty, hollow, wasted delusion."

The Word of God must be our basis for truth! *Faith cannot rest upon your experience, my experience or any other person's experience.* Faith must rest entirely upon the written Word of God.

Let Him be Accursed

I am very aware that the kind of stand I am taking on this point is unpopular with some people. However, it was this very same stand that Paul took when he responded to the error invading the church of Galatia.

Because false revelators were teaching things that were

in opposition to the gospel of grace, and because they were actually adding new revelations to Paul's message which were not in agreement with the Word that Paul preached, Paul said, "But though we, or an angel from heaven, preach any other gospel unto you than that which we have preached unto you, *let him be accursed."*

To make sure his voice is heard, he repeats himself again, "As we said before, so say I now again, If any man preach any other gospel unto you than that ye have received from me, *let him be accursed"* (Galatians 1:8-9).

What did Paul mean when he said, *"let him be accursed?"*

The word "accursed" is from the Greek word *anathema* (ana-the-ma), and it specifically means "let him be abandoned by God, and doomed to destruction."

Knowing that he was not winning any brownie points with some people for making these strong, straightforward statements, Paul continued to say, "For do I now persuade men or God? Or do I seek to please men? For if I yet pleased men, I should not be the servant of Christ" (Galatians 1:10).

Paul did not care if the bogus prophets and teachers of his day approved or disapproved of him. He was not in a popularity contest. *The issue at stake was the Word of God.*

He could have shut his eyes and ignored the problem; and he could have opted for silence in regard to these serious doctrinal aberations. This silent route would have certainly kept him in good graces with the fraudulent leaders.

However, he knew that if he shut his eyes to these problems and did not speak up in order to protect the gospel of grace and the Church, he would cease to be the servant of God, and would instead have become a man-pleaser.

Thus, the reason he said, "For if I yet pleased men, I should not be the servant of Christ."

Colossian Angel Worshippers

Before we move to our fifth important point in Colossians 2:18, first we must see how critical the error in

Colosse was becoming. Paul continues, "Let no man beguile you of your reward through a voluntary humility and *worshipping of angels. . . .*"

Though he does not tells us how it came to pass, Paul informs us that the Colossian church had somehow began practicing the worship of angels. This perversion may have begun with some leader in the church who had experienced a genuine encounter with an angel. Though we are not certain, this *may* have been the case.

Regardless of how this worship of angels first began in the Colossian church, *it is very clear that they had angels on the mind.*

According to Church history, Gnostic prophets and teachers were all the time giving new names to angels, and even attempted to form lineages for various angelic family lines. From the context of Paul's epistles, it appears that this is the *very* type of error that had gotten a foothold in the Colossian church.

In fact, this fascination with angels eventually became so far-fetched, that they began to "worship" angels. "Worship" is from the Greek word *threskeia* (thres-kei-a), and it depicts the literal act of "worship" and "service" to some brand of religion.

The fact that Paul would use a "worship" word to describe the intensity of their error, means these weird experiences and revelations were no longer on the outer fringe of the church. Instead, they were right smack in the midst of the church family; so accepted that these spiritual aberations were being "serviced" by the leaders and people.

This would have never occurred if the Word of God had been used as a check and balance to judge these things.

Spiritual Egomaniacs

Paul continues once again, "Let no man beguile you of your reward through a voluntary humility and worshipping of angels, intruding into those things which he hath not seen, *vainly puffed up by his fleshly mind."*

Notice the fifth important point in this verse. Paul says this kind of person is, "vainly puffed up by his fleshly mind."

The phrase "vainly puffed up" is from the Greek word *phusioo* (phu-si-oo), and it characterizes a person who is so impressed with his own sense of greatness, that he has become mentally "bloated." The word *phusioo* literally describes someone who is "puffed up, blown up" or "mentally inflated."

By using this word, Paul tells us in *the strongest of words* that though these fraudulent ministries may attempt to put on the outward disguise of humility, inwardly they are incredible *egomaniacs.*

This egotistical spiritual pride may be kept under cover for a period of time. As a matter of fact, it will probably never outwardly manifest unless the prophet or teacher that is in question, is requested to scripturally prove their experience.

This is normally when the outward facade of humility falls off a deceived leader, and a raging, angry, prideful carnality manifests. *"What do you mean?" "Are you questioning me?" "How dare you question my anointing!" "Who do you think you are?"*

Submission to a Local Church and Pastor

If a prophet or teacher cannot submit to authority, specifically to a local church and a local pastor, then they should *not* be ministering in the pulpit.

The Bible plainly teaches that submission to authority is the foundation for usefulness. Paul said, "Now he which established us with you in Christ, and hath anointed us, is God" (Second Corinthians 1:21).

Notice that before Paul ever mentions the anointing, first he says he was "established." The word "established" is the word *bebaios* (be-bai-os), and it refers to being consistent and faithful in the basest, most elementary and foundational things.

If a traveling minister cannot be faithful to a local church or a pastor, then he is not ready for a heavy anointing. His track records shows that he or she is not really tested, proven or submitted.

This kind of person may walk in the pretense of submission to a church and pastor for a period of time. But if he or she has something, such as a new experience or revelation, that their pastor questions, this is normally when he or she will show their true colors.

This is nearly always the golden moment when this person feels "led to join another church." That is when the church and pastor realize that this person has walked only in a "mock submission."

If a prophet or teacher will not submit their new doctrine or revelation to pastoral authority in their lives, then it is safe to assume that the minister who will not submit, probably questions the validity of the experience himself. The reason he cannot submit is because he knows that if his new doctrine is brought under scrutiny, it will be discredited by the Word of God.

You must also know that a false revelation causes people to be prideful about their own spirituality. This is the very reason that Paul says they are "puffed up, blown up" and have a "bloated" perspective of themselves.

Chapter Ten
Typhoons, Disease, War and Self-Hypnosis

Y̶ou may be asking, "What in the world do typhoons, disease, war and self-hypnosis have to do with each other?"

According to Paul's word in First Timothy 6:4-5, these are perfect descriptions of how a false prophet or false teacher will behave.

In First Timothy 6:4-5, Paul says, "He is proud, knowing nothing, but doting about questions and strifes of words, whereof cometh envy, strife, railings, evil surmisings, perverse disputings of men of corrupt minds, and destitute of the truth, supposing that gain is godliness: from such withdraw thyself."

In this jammed-packed verse, the apostle Paul gives us twelve very important and utterly undiluted characterizations about how false prophets and false teachers carry on in their ministries.

Because this verse is so detailed and important to this subject, we will deal with each of these extremely important points one at a time in this chapter.

Notice first of all, that when Paul describes the behavior of these misguided individuals, he tops this terrible list with "pride." In First Timothy 6:4, Paul says, *"He is proud. . . ."*

The word "proud" in Greek is from the word *tuphuoo* (tu-phuoo). This is perhaps one of the most dramatic illustrations that Paul could have ever given us on this subject of

123

erroneous behavior in the ministry. Why?

In the first place, the word *tuphuoo* was used in a very demeaning sense to depict a person "who is so completely preoccupied by his own sense of spiritual greatness, that he has become puffed up." Or you could say that this word *tuphuoo* describes someone who is " wrapped up in the smoke of self-deception."

The whole idea is that these persons have become so impressed by their own spirituality, that they have lost touch altogether with the real world, and now they see themselves as something that they really are not.

This kind of person is so very dangerous to the life of the local church, that Paul uses this very word in First Timothy 3:6, when he says, "Not a novice, lest being lifted up with pride he fall into the condemnation of the devil."

This phrase, "lifted up with pride," is also taken from the word *tuphuoo*. However, notice that in this particular verse, Paul goes on to tell us what has caused this person "to be lifted up with pride."

From the context of this verse, it is clear that it is a drastic mistake to place a newcomer into important places of ministry and leadership too quickly. Unfortunately, this is a lesson which most of us have learned the hard way.

Something strange happens to the mind when it tastes authority and power — and especially if it tastes authority and power too quickly.

If a person is promoted and elevated into lofty positions of authority too quickly, it can open a door for the devil to come in and create false delusions of spiritual grandeur for that individual.

There is no doubt that it is spiritually detrimental to promote a newcomer *too quickly*. After being quickly inducted into the leadership of a church, it is possible for that newcomer to become so impressed by his or her spiritual advancement, that they may begin to think they are something very "extra special."

The Example of Lucifer

This is the very reason that Paul commanded Timothy, "Not a novice, lest being lifted up with pride he fall into the condemnation of the devil."

The word "condemnation" is the Greek word *krima* (kri-ma), and it is understood to carry the idea of a "verdict, judgment" or "sentence." This is exactly the point which Paul is making in this pivotal verse about leadership.

Paul is clearly warning us that if one is elevated too quickly into a place of notoriety in the ministry, you are placing this person in a position to be tempted in the same way that Lucifer was tempted.

In fact, because Paul uses the word "condemnation" (*krima*), he is actually alerting us to the fact that to promote and elevate a man or woman's ministry too quickly, nearly always releases the verdict of Lucifer's own failure upon them.

What does this mean?

Paul is obviously referring to Lucifer's own self-deception and false delusions of granduer.

Lucifer, if not *the* most beautiful creature God ever made, was certainly one of the most beautiful creatures God made. As a matter of fact, he was so beautiful and resplendent, that he became "wrapped in smoke" in regard to his own importance.

So impressed was he by his own beauty, that he said, "I will ascend into heaven, I will exalt my throne above the stars of God: I will sit upon the mount of the congregation, in the sides of the north: I will ascend above the heights of the clouds; I will be like the most High" (Isaiah 14:13-14).

His perspective of himself was so unrealisitic and bloated, that he actually began to slander and attack God Himself. When God cast him forth from heaven, He identified the root of Lucifer's deception when He said, "Thine heart was lifted

125

up because of thy beauty, thou hast corrupted thy wisdom by reason of thy brightness. . ." (Ezekiel 28:17).

It seems that this is the very picture that Paul has in mind when he says, "Not a novice, lest being lifted up with pride he fall into the condemnation of the devil."

Paul knew that by elevating an individual too quickly into prominent places of ministry in the Body of Christ, we put them into a position to be self-deceived about their own spirituality. And this is just the beginning of trouble.

If they become infatuated with their own sense of spiritual greatness, it will not be too long until they, like Lucifer, begin to view themselves as being greater than the very church leadership who first promoted them.

If this unrealisitic view of themselves begins to take root in their hearts — thus *"wrapping them up in the smoke of self-deception"* — this deceived leader will begin to attack and slander others in the same manner that Lucifer attempted to attack and slander God.

This is clearly the reason that Paul tells us not to allow a "novice" to move into leadership positions too quickly.

This prohibition is not meant to be a heavy restriction upon the newcomer; but rather, a protection for the newcomer. By delaying their elevation into prominent positions, we are guarding them against a deception that would try to overtake them.

Typhoons in the Ministry

It is also very interesting to note that the word *tuphuoo* is where we get the word "typhoon." There is no doubt that this conveys yet another serious and important message to us.

If a person is elevated too quickly into notable places of ministry, you may be releasing a typhoon or hurricane into your life! This will be especially true if he or she falls into the condemnation of the devil, or into the same pattern that the devil fell into (i.e., attacking and slandering authorities).

If they become "wrapped in smoke" and "puffed up" by their own unrealistic sense of greatness, they may release incredible amounts of turbulence into the local church. Unfortunately, this is another lesson which most of us have learned the hard way.

So when Paul characterized these individuals and said, "He is proud," he is conveying a powerful message and warning to the church about advancing people too hastily.

False prophets and false teachers, if given a place of prominence in the Body of Christ, will move across the church with tremendous force, destroying everything in their path as they move along with *typhoon proportions.*

Therefore, it is wiser to wait and allow a person to mature before being promoted and lifted up into a place of authority. *Many good people have been destroyed because they were placed too high, too fast.*

None of us are above being tempted in this area of pride and self-deception.

"Hurricane Saul"

Had the weather bureau been active during the early days of the church, they probably would have called the squall that Paul created, "Hurricane Saul," since he still bore that name at the time.

When first saved and called by God, the scripture teaches us that Saul immediately tried to elevate himself into leadership ranks in the church of Jerusalem. He was still such a young convert when he tried to do this, that the leaders there were not yet certain that he was even genuinely saved.

Acts 9:26 says, "And when Saul was come to Jerusalem, he assayed to join himself to the disciples: but they were afraid of him, and believed not that he was a disciple."

By studying Acts, chapter 9, it is clear that initially only Barnabas believed his conversion story. Finally, with

Barnabas' stamp of approval and help, he was received by the brethren in Jerusalem.

However, this was not the end of problems for the young convert. From the typhoon situation that Saul created in the city, it is apparent that he tried to force his way into public ministry immediately after his conversion.

During this time, he himself proved to be quite a typhoon for the brethren. As a young, untested and unfounded New Testament believer, he stirred up such hatred and animosity against the Grecians, that they desired to have him killed.

The whole ordeal became so volatile, that "when the brethren knew of it, they brought him down to Caesarea, and sent him forth to Tarsus" (verse 30). In other words, they put him on a boat and sent him home!

The scripture declares, "Then had the churches rest throughout all Judaea and Galilee and Samaria. . . ." (verse 31).

Though Paul had great zeal for the Lord, the results of his behavior turned out to be more like the activity of a *typhoon.* Like a strong wind that destroys everything in their path, his unchecked zeal was damaging the church.

Had he been allowed to continue in this course of action without correction, there is no doubt that serious flaws would have developed in his life and ministry. He simply was not ready for this type of spiritual promotion at that early time.

Because the elders of Jerusalem understood the importance of waiting before a person is promoted into important public positions, the disciples sent him home to learn the basics at the church in Tarsus.

Because Paul was so well acquainted with the dangers of "being lifted up with pride," he is very qualified to begin his twelve point list of character flaws here with this first point: *"pride."*

Let us not be guilty of destroying potentially good ministries by elevating them *too high, too fast.*

Experts at Nothing

But Paul does not stop here with this first point. He goes on to mention the second point about these potentially dangerous individuals.

Concerning them and their revelations, Paul says, they *"know nothing. . . ."*

What a contrast this is to what these revelators were claiming! Why? Because these sinister ministers *claimed to know everything.*

The phrase "knowing nothing" is taken from the Greek phrase *meden epistamenos* (me-den epi-sta-me-nos). The word *epistamenos* actually describes a person who possesses an "expertise" in some area. They know their subject matter inside and out. Therefore, by using this word, Paul is calling these individuals "experts."

However, notice what he says their realm of expertise is about. He uses the word *meden* to make his point. The word *meden* is one of the strongest words you can find in the Greek to describe "nothing."

So when you take these two words together, Paul plainly tells us that false prophets and false teachers, though they make many great claims of spirituality and carry on as though they have insight that no one else possesses, are in reality "experts at nothing."

In other words, though they "speak great swelling words of vanity" (Second Peter 2:18) and over-emphasize the depth of their spiritual perception, thus carrying on as though they are great spiritual experts, Paul says they are "experts at nothing."

Their words are nothing more than hot air.

A Terminal Disease

Then Paul makes his third point about these doctrinal

troublemakers. He says these types of leaders are always *"doting about questions. . . ."*

The word "doting" is taken from the Greek word *nosos* (no-sos), which is used throughout the Gospels of the New Testament to describe individuals who were "terminally afflicted with a disease for which there is no natural cure."

The picture conveyed here is the graphic illustration of a person who has a disease similar to terminal cancer or AIDS.

Because of the serious nature of these terminal illnesses, the victim is left utterly hopeless for recovery and a return to normalcy, unless God intervenes with a supernatural miracle of deliverance and healing.

By utilizing this illustration, Paul means to tell us that *the majority of false prophets and false teachers are inwardly afflicted with a terminal spiritual disease for which there is no cure.* It is clear that these to whom Paul is referring, are so terminally afflicted, that only a miracle from God will bring them out of this bondage and deception.

One expositor has said this is the portrayal of a minister with *a morbid preoccupation with deadly things.* What things is this afflicted minister preoccupied with?

Paul tells us. He says this individual is "doting *about questions. . . ."*

The word "questions" illustrates for us once again the extent to which these ministers have become diseased. "Questions" is from the word *zetesis* (ze-te-sis), and it describes a "theorizing about things which cannot be substantiated."

In plain language, this tells us that false prophets and false teachers love to delve into things that do not really matter. They are so consumed with these non-life-changing issues, that this is all they want to talk about, preach about or prophesy about.

This is the picture of a hopeless addict, going from one thing to another, then another and another in pursuit of a superficial "high." Looking for something that no one else has ever heard or found, they are on *an endless treadmill* in pursuit of revelation that does not satisfy or make a difference in anyone's life.

The only way these people will ever be healed and brought back into a circumspect spiritual walk, is if they receive a sovereign touch from God to set them free from this sickness.

The sovereign touch of healing and deliverance which these spiritually afflicted people desperately need, is available to them if they would only recognize their need for it and open their heart to receive it from heaven.

Even a physically ill, medical patient cannot be helped unless he recognizes his need for treatment. Though the medical facilities and treatments for his total healing are available, they will only begin to work for him when he acknowledges his need and seeks help.

Deception is so strong and so deep, that only a supernatural miracle will set a spiritually diseased person free. This miracle is set in motion for their deliverance when the need for it is acknowledged and sought after.

A War of Words

However, Paul tells us that rather than seeking help for their spiritual affliction, most of these afflicted leaders have a way of going from bad to worse.

In fact, their morbid preoccupation with the unimportant eventually becomes so gross, that they will even "fight" over these issues with each other.

This is the reason that Paul now mentions his fourth point. He tells us these error-ridden, doctrinal troublemakers are always "doting about questions *and strifes of words. . . .*"

The phrase "strifes of words" comes from the Greek

compound *logomachia* (lo-go-mach-ia). *Logo* (lo-go) is from the word *logos* (lo-gos), and it simply means "words." *Machia* (mach-ia) is from *machomai* (macho-mai), and it depicts "war, bloodshed" and "intense fighting."

When these two words are compounded together, they depict the hostile, ugly, violent behavior of people who are "verbally fighting each other with words."

There is no situation more volatile than the situation which develops when two supposed spiritual "know-it-alls" meet together to wrangle over their new revelations.

According to Paul's words in this text, the deception that has possessed these infected leaders is so deeply rooted that they will literally go to "war" with each other in order to prove that their insight and revelation is *spiritually superior* to the other's.

A Natural Sequence of Events

Then Paul very quickly lumps the next four points about the behavior of rebellious prophets and teachers all together as though they are a natural chain of events.

Very hastily and without delay, Paul tells us that "envy, strife, railings and evil surmisings" are the fruit of each other. One of these expressions always gives place to the next. Paul says, "whereof cometh envy, strife, railings and evil surmisings."

"Envy," the fifth character flaw in these individuals, comes from the Greek word *phthonos* (ph-tho-nos), and it describes "competition, jealousy" or "ambition."

It is so vile that we find it listed as a "work of the flesh" in Galatians 5:21. If this "work of the flesh" is active in the life of a leader, you can be absolutely certain *on the basis of scripture and experience*, that this will naturally lead into the next expression in this chain of events: *"strife."*

A Party Spirit Inside the church

The word "strife" leads us to the sixth character flaw of

these deceived prophets and teachers.

The word "strife" used in this particular verse, is from the little, but powerful Greek word, *eris*. The word *eris* is used on many occasions in the New Testament to denote the idea of "division," "a faction," or even "a party spirit." It is this idea of "a party spirit" that primarily concerns Paul's usage of it in First Timothy 6:4.

Eris is taken from the word *ereithia*, which first was used to depict different political factions with different political agendas and platforms. Like political parties today, each party believed that their platform and agenda was correct; therefore, they were willing to fight each other in order to promote their own ideas.

We find this word *eris* ("strifes" or "party spirit") used in this very way in First Corinthians 1:11, where Paul uses it to describe "a party spirit" that was developing inside the church of Corinth over the issue of leadership.

This "party spirit" in Corinth progressively became so bad, that the church ended up miserably divided. As Paul said, "Now this I say, that every one of you saith, I am of Paul; and I of Apollos; and I of Cephas; and I am of Christ. *Is Christ divided?*" (First Corinthians 1:12-13).

To let us know the extent of this "party spirit" that grew in the church of Corinth, Paul asked them, *"Is Christ divided?"*

The word "divided" is from the word *meridzo* (me-rid-zo), and it is used in the perfect tense, indicating that Christ in this city, had already been torn, ripped, shredded to pieces, divided and distributed out to different groups of differing opinions within the same church.

With this in mind, Paul tells us that conflicts with false prophets and false teachers have a way of naturally deteriorating. Things do not get better with them. Once again, they have a way of going from bad to worse.

There is a proper, scriptural time to divide from fellowshipping with others. For instance, in Second Thessalonians

3:6, Paul says, "withdraw yourselves from every brother that walketh disorderly among you."

He continues in verse 14, "And if any man obey not our word by this epistle, note that man and have no company with him, that he may be ashamed."

It is very clear that there are occasions when the Word of God commands us to separate ourselves from people who walk in error. However, that is not what Paul is speaking of in First Timothy 6:4, when he mentions "strife."

The division that he is describing isn't a result of integrity and commitment to the Word of God. Rather, this is a division that results from ambition and competition.

Once this ungodly "envy" has begun to work in the Church, like political parties of differing opinions, people begin to divide up into different groups with whom they agree!

From the vantage of their own peculiar group; and functioning in a negative, divisive, factioned manner; willing to fight in order to promote their own ideas, even to the exclusion of the rights of others; they immediately begin to manifest the next character flaw in this sequence of events: *"railings."*

Railings and Blasphemies

Paul moves to his seventh point about the behavior of misguided, fraudulent prophets and teachers. They begin to "rail" one another!

The word "railings" tells us what these deceived people *do* to each other! The word "railings" comes from the word *blasphemeo* (blas-phe-meo), and this is where we obtain the word "blasphemy."

Though most people try to spiritualize "blasphemy" and think of it as something that is linked only to "the blasphemy of the Holy Spirit" (Matthew 12:31-32), there are many forms of "blasphemy" besides this.

The word "blasphemy" simply means "to injure" or "to hurt someone with cruel, unkind words."

By using this word at this juncture of his statement about the behavior of spiritual troublemakers, Paul tells us that once these people have divided up into their different camps of differing opinions, and "a party spirit" begins to develop, then they begin to hurl insults at each other.

This leads toward the next step of degeneration in this process: *"evil surmisings."*

Self-Hypnosis

You may ask, "How in the world can anyone treat the Body of Christ like this, and do it with a clear conscience?"

Paul indicates that the deception they have imposed upon themselves is so strong, that they have come under a type of *hypnosis.*

The word "surmisings" is from the Greek compound word, *huponoeo* (hu-po-no-eo). The word *hupo* (hu-po) means "under," and the word *noeo* (no-eo) is from the word *nous,* which is the Greek word for the "mind."

When these two words are compounded together, they portray a person who is "under the control of his own mind." This is precisely where we get the word "hypnosis."

By electing to use this word, Paul is telling us that individuals who carry on this way — *abusing the church and ripping the Word of God to shreds* — are under some type of mesmerizing spell. The notion is implied that these particular people genuinely believe that their behavior, attitudes and conduct is right.

(For more on this self-deception, see pages 152-156 in my book, SEDUCING SPIRITS AND DOCTRINES OF DEMONS).

Perverse Disputings

Then Paul tells us what these characters are like when

you get them all together in one room! For his ninth point in this horrendous list, he says they are given to *"perverse disputings."*

What a word! "Perverse disputings" is from the word *diaparatribe* (dia-pa-ra-tri-be), and it is a tripple compound of the words *dia, para* and *tribe.*

Dia conveys the idea of "penetration," *para* denotes a very close, side-by-side relationship, and *tribe* depicts something that is extremely "irritating."

When all three are taken together as one complete word, they describe "a terrible, irritating, prolonged wrangling and quarreling that begins to incite the worst of human passions."

In fact, this irritation of the flesh becomes so prolonged and involved, that eventually these pseudo ministers begin to "rub each other the wrong way" and eventually "penetrate" each other with the vilest of attitudes.

Corrupt Minds

Then Paul plainly tells us "why" false prophets and false teachers carry on the way they do. For his tenth point in this text, he declares to us that they have *"corrupt minds."*

The word "corrupt" is taken from the Greek word *diaphtheiro* (diaph-thei-ro). It describes something that is utterly corrupted from one side to the other. This is not merely *a tainted mind;* this is *a totally depraved mind.*

However, these deceived ministers did not start out this way. This is the reason that Paul continues to tells us that they are *"destitute of the truth."*

Destitute of the Truth

The word "destitute," *apostereo,* (pronounced a-po-stereo) literally means "to rob, steal" or "to deprive."

The very fact that Paul uses this word to illustrate them, tells us that at one prior time these individuals *did* have a firm

136

grasp upon the truth of God's Word. Since that earlier time, however, the truth has been taken from them.

How was the truth taken from them? How were they "deprived" of the truth?

By virtue of their own will to go their own way, and by ignoring the pleadings of the Holy Spirit to correct their teachings, their attitudes and their behavior, they have "seared their consciences with a hot iron."

In other words, because of their willful disobedience to the truth of God's Word and their blatant, outright refusal to submit themselves to this truth, they have cauterized their spirits — so that they can no longer distinguish between what is right and what is wrong.

Therefore, for Paul's eleventh point, he tells us that these kinds of backslidden leaders, who once had a firm grasp upon the truth, have sinced stripped themselves of the truth because of their own lifestyle and conduct.

Justifying Willful Disobedience

Yet, it is clear from Paul's words that these frauds continue to be financially blessed in spite of their activities. This leads us to Paul's twelfth point.

He says that these deceived leaders *"suppose that gain is godliness."*

What does this mean?

This means that when they are confronted by other leaders who are concerned about their actions, teachings and behavior, rather than hear the truth, submit to it and change, they say, *"Hey, I must be doing something right! My offerings have never been bigger, I've never had more partners, and the money has never been more abundant! You can say what you want to say about me, but it is hard to argue with success."*

However, the truth of the matter is that the Body of Christ has supported many frauds and counterfeits throughout history. Even Peter, in Second Peter 2:2, was amazed by this phenomena of people supporting bad ministries. He said, "Many shall follow their pernicious ways. . . ."

The reasons people follow this kind of ministry are abundant. (We will cover some of these in Chapter 13). However, outward success is not always a sign of spiritual success.

I cannot help but think of Jesus' words to the great Ephesian church. In Revelation 2:5, Jesus said, "Remember, therefore, from whence thou art fallen, and repent and do the first works. . . ."

This was the famous, huge Ephesian church that Jesus was addressing! The church of Ephesus, with all of it's quirks and problems, was still viewed to be the most spiritual, solid, stable church during this period of history. Yet, to this solid, stable, mature church, Jesus says, "Remember, therefore, from whence *thou art fallen. . . .*"

The word "fallen" is in the perfect active indicative tense and indicates the idea of a "completed downfall." Therefore, Jesus is not predicting a possible future spiritual decline, but rather, he is speaking about a "completed downfall" which has *already* occurred.

What a shock this must have been to the ears of the Ephesian church. In the eyes of men, they were the pinnacle of spiritual maturity and stability. Yet, when the Lord addresses this huge, outwardly successful church, he says,"*thou art fallen.*"

Outward success cannot be our measure of true success in God. If this were the case, then the majority of prophets in the Old Testament were utter failures, for they never had the approval of man.

If outward success is the measure of success in God, then John the Baptist, the apostle Paul, Peter and others in the New Testament were also utter failures. *Neither did they have the approval of man.* In addition to this void of man's approval during their ministries, when they departed this world, they had but a handful of friends who had remained faithful to them.

Technically, if outward success is the genuine measure of our success in God, then *Jesus Himself* never achieved spiritual success.

Though the Lord may have temporarily enjoyed the favor of huge crowds who followed him from place to place, he did not die with the favor of the multitudes upon him and his ministry. Instead, he died between two criminals, public offenders, and suffered the ultimate shame and public disgrace: *death on a cross.*

Yet, Paul tells us that false prophets and false teachers base their success on how much money they are receiving, how big their crowds are, how large their mailing list is, etc. *They suppose that material gain is the evidence of God's approval.*

While we thank God for his material blessings that abound on our ministries and lives, we cannot let these outward things be our guide for godly success.

This is the reason Paul ended this text by commanding us very sharply, "From such withdraw thyself."

This must not be our measure of spiritual success in God!

139

Chapter Eleven
The Ultimate Experience

Peter's description of false prophets and false teachers in Second Peter 2:1-22, is the strongest, lengthiest picture of them in the New Testament.

His characterization of them is so impassioned, that he likens them unto "dogs who eat their own vomit," and "pigs who wallow in the mire" (Second Peter 2:22).

However, before he begins his unabashed protrayal of them and their fictional ministries, he first backs up and declares that they are not the only ones who have supernatural stories to tell. *He confesses that he has had some amazing, genuine supernatural experiences himself.*

The difference between Peter's story and theirs? Peter's supernatural encounter wasn't a fabricated tale he conjured up in order to captivate the ear of the people. *His story was real!*

Thus the reason that Peter said, "For we have not followed cunningly devised fables when we made known unto you the power and coming of our Lord Jesus Christ."

Refusing to Behave Wrongly

Before Peter tells his readers about his famous, supernatural experience on the Mount of Transfiguration with Jesus, he first clearly wants to separate himself from others who told blatant lies about their own spiritual adventures.

By saying, "We have not followed cunningly devised

fables," Peter is conveying two very important messages to his readers: *1) he wants his readers to know how false ministries behave and carry on in their ministries,* and *2) he wants his readers to know absolutely and emphatically that he has refused to behave this way in his ministry.*

In the first place, Peter says, "We have *not followed. . . ."*

The word "followed" is taken from the Greek word *exakoloutheo* (ex-a-ko-lou-theo). The first part of the word, *koloutheo,* means "to follow." This would normally have been sufficient to make Peter's point in this verse.

However, because Peter didn't feel this was strong enough, he added the prefix *ex* to the first of the word, which adds to the word the feeling of *domination, force, determination or the idea of aggression.*

Therefore, the word "follow," isn't simply the notion of leisurely following along after something, but rather, this is the idea of *"chasing after something with all of your might, pursuing an object with an unrelenting force,"* or *"aggressively tracking something down, in order to capture it and make it your own."*

However, when Peter used this word, he used it in a negative context. He said, "we have *not* followed. . . ." The idea is, "we have not chased after, pursued and given ourselves over to this kind of spiritual approach."

By making this statement, he is incriminating some of the other fellow ministers with whom he is familiar. The insinuation is that some of the leaders he is acquainted with are taking an outlandish spiritual approach to things. Like other off-base ministers of that day, they had given themselves over to weird experiences and outlandish revelations.

Peter refuses — *absolutely refuses* — to participate in this type of foolish and outrageous behavior. Therefore, in this verse he separates himself from them! This is denial and disassociation! He wants his readers to know that he is not like them; he is not a spiritual hallucinator!

Thus he says, "we have not followed, pursued or aggressively chased. . . ." Then he tells us what some are "chasing after." He says they are chasing after "cunningly devised fables. . . ."

Cunningly Devised Fables

By using the phrase "cunningly devised fables," Peter is telling us exactly what he thinks of some of his peers' stories.

The phrase "cunningly devised" is from the word *sophidzo* (so-phid-zo), and it describes something that is "cleverly contrived, made-up, concocted, fabricated" or "invented."

According to his view of things, these Gnostic revelators didn't possess new revelation. In the truest sense of the word, all they possessed were stories which they had "concocted" and "made-up."

Their mythical stories eventually became extremely elongated, terribly exaggerated and completely out-of-balance. In order to cover discrepancies in their stories and teachings, they went to the Word to locate scriptures which they could use to substantiate their experiences. With these in hand, they began to frame brand new, never-before-heard, off-the-wall doctrines to accompany their revelations and to validate them as truth.

It is clear even to the casual reader and student, that the Word of God had become *secondary*, and experience had become *preeminent* in many circles of the Church.

On account of this utter spiritual foolishness, Peter seems to tell us, "As far as I'm concerned, what they are teaching is nothing more than a bunch of fictitious, contrived, made-up, concocted and fabricated stories. . . ."

Regardless of what they were doing in their meetings, or how popular they were becoming with the masses, Peter says, "*Not me!*" He continues by saying, "we have not followed cunningly devised *fables*. . . ."

Unrestrained, Far-stretched Teaching

The word "fables" is from the Greek word *muthos* (mu-thos) and is the same root from which we derive the word "mythology."

Quite literally, the word "myth" describes something that has been "fantasized, imagined, dreamed-up" or is "make-believe."

By using this word to describe his peers' activities, Peter is telling us just how off-base some of his peers had become! According to his words in this verse, their teaching was so crazy and off-the-wall that it really came much closer to mythology than it did to the Word of God.

He is driving his point right into the hearts of his readers!

There is no question about it, Peter believed some of the stories being told by others were nothing more than a lot of made-up, concocted, fictitious experiences.

The word "fables," which Peter uses, is used throughout the New Testament. Paul used it in First Timothy 1:4 when he told Timothy, "Neither give heed to fables and endless genealogies. . . ."

He used it again in First Timothy 4:7 when he said, "But refuse profane and old wives' tales. . . ." The word "tales" is also from the word *muthos* which is where we get the word "fables".

From these two examples in First Timothy, we are able to determine several things about spiritual "fables" and "tales."

First, notice that Paul connects the word "fables" with "endless genealogies" in First Timothy 1:4. The phrase "endless genealogies" is extremely significant, because it demonstrates just how far off a teaching can become.

The word "endless" is from the word *aperantos* (a-pe-ran-tos), and it vividly speaks of something that knows "no restraint" or "limitation." Therefore, this refers to something that is "uncontrollable, unrestrained, far-fetched" and "way-off-base."

By using this word, Paul confirms for us once again that *spiritual lunacy has a way of going from bad to worse.*

If these prophets, teachers and newfangled doctrines are not corrected and brought back into balance, they will become utterly "uncontrollable" and "unrestrained." There is no limit to the excess that off-base believers can enter into!

To alert us to what these "unrestrained revelations" ultimately produce in a believer's life, Paul calls them "profane and old wives' tales" (First Timothy 4:7).

The word "profane" is from the word *bebelos* (be-be-los). It denotes something that is so nasty and contemptible that it shouldn't be allowed inside your home. Instead, you must pick this up and pitch it out into the street where it belongs! As time went on, the word "profane" actually came to describe "manure!"

What does this tell us about "cunningly devised fables?"

It tells us that these things do not belong in our spiritual lives any more than manure belongs in your living room!

If you permit these unrestrained revelations and strange manifestations to have an important role in your life, you will eventually have quite a "stinking" problem to deal with and to correct in your life or the life of your church!

A Play on Words

Peter continues, "we have not followed cunningly devised fables *when we made known unto you. . . .*"

The word "known" is from the word *gnosis* (gno-sis), which we covered very thoroughly in Chapter 8. As we saw in Chapter 8, it means "knowledge" and is the word from which the Gnostics obtained their name.

By using this word at this juncture in this verse, Peter is implying two important things to us.

145

First of all, there is no doubt that by using the word *gnosis*, Peter is alluding to the super-spirituals he has run into over the years who claim to possess "special knowledge."

He dangles the word *gnosis* out in front of these spiritually elite, as if to say, *"If you want to talk about knowledge, then listen to what I'm about to say. . . ."*

Secondly, by using the word *gnosis*, he tells us that, unlike others who boasted of special knowledge — but had none — he truly has been endowed with an experience that elevated his spiritual insight and understanding above others.

Along with James and John, Peter has had a genuine experience that supersedes anyone's wildest expectations!

The Mount of Transfiguration

He continues, ". . .when we made known unto you the power and coming of our Lord Jesus Christ, but were eyewitnesses of his majesty."

Notice, first of all, that Peter begins his true story by mentioning "the power and coming of our Lord Jesus Christ."

The word "power" is from the word *dunamis* (du-na-mis). The word *dunamis* is a well-known and often-used Greek word that describes unbelievable, explosively powerful "strength" and "ability." This is where the word "dynamite" comes from.

As Peter relates his experience on the mountain top to us, he can still vividly remember what it felt like to be there when the awesome power of Jesus Christ permeated his entire being that day.

According to Matthew's account of this visitation in Matthew 17:6, this "strength" was so strong and overwhelming that "they fell on their faces, and were sore afraid."

You must keep in mind that this was not Peter's first encounter with power.

He had seen Jesus heal the sick, cast out demons, walk on water, multiply food and even raise the dead. Yet, he had never observed *this type of power*.

That day the veil of the flesh and the spirit was parted for Peter, James and John. For the first time, they saw Jesus as no other earthly eye had ever seen Him — in all of His matchless, marvelous, power, strength and ability!

He continues, "when we made known unto you the power and *coming* of our Lord Jesus Christ."

The word "coming" is taken from the Greek word parousia (par-ou-sia). Theologians have used this word to describe the Lord's soon return. However, this is not the meaning which Peter conveys to us in this verse.

The word *parousia* is a compound of the word *para* and the word *ousia*. *Para* is a preposition that means "along" or "alongside of," and the word *ousia* in its most literal sense means "to be." When these words are compounded together, they mean" to personally be alongside of." In other words, this describes a first-hand encounter, or a "personal experience."

Because Peter uses this word when chronicling his encounter with the Lord on the Mount of Transfiguration, we know that this experience was still very fresh in his mind. He is still deeply moved when he considers the fact that he was "personally there" when this event occurred.

This is a deeply moving and personal experience which Peter is sharing with us. He was there; he saw this happen; he personally felt the awesome power of God; he basked in the radiant glory; and heard God's audible voice with his very own ears.

What an experience to remember!

By now, the false revelators whom Peter has been confronting through his letter must have been sitting on the edge of their seats. This was *the ultimate supernatural experience!*

This was the very thing they had always wanted to experience!

Eyewitnesses of His Majesty

Still awe-struck by this occurrence on the mountain top, Peter now begins to unfold his exciting story to us sequence-by-sequence.

Filled with reminiscent memories of this glorious moment, he says, "we were eyewitnesses of his majesty."

The word "eyewitnesses" is from the word *epoptes* (ep-op-tes). It literally means "to look on" and describes a "bystander." This is a reference to a person who had "personally witnessed something with his own eyes."

It was also used as a religious word among pagan cults. Pagan mystery religions were very secretive. Only a small elite group of individuals were allowed into the higher levels of their secretive societies.

To become a part of the higher echelon of the religion, it was required that you first go through a "rite of initiation." If you were *not* willing to "look on" and take part in the initiation, thus becoming a participant, then you were not allowed to go any higher into the society.

On the other hand, those who were willing to "look on" were "initiated" because of what they had seen and heard in those secret quarters. Their new knowledge made them participants in the deeper secrets of their religion. Thus, they were inducted into the higher, most spiritual class of their religious community.

Since this is the background for the word "eyewitnesses," it is clear that Peter is telling us, *"I've had an experience with the Lord that only a small handful in history have ever experienced. Because of the rarity of this occurrence, I have been truly inducted into a special, elite group of three — James, John and myself. Only we three have seen Jesus in this powerful way!"*

In the truest sense of the word, Peter can say that he has seen what no other eye has ever seen; he has heard what no other ear has ever heard; and he has gone boldly where no other man has ever gone!

Beholding the Majesty of Jesus Christ

The false prophets and false teachers must have been drooling on themselves as they listened to this episode that Peter was sharing. They knew that his story was real!

Here was everything they desired in a supernatural experience! Supernatural power, a divine encounter, and an "initiation" into a group of specially privileged people!

Yet, with all of this exposure and experience under his belt, notice what stands out foremost in Peter's mind when he recalls his experience. He says, "we were eyewitnesses of *his majesty.*"

The word "majesty" comes from the word *megaleiotes* (me-ga-lei-o-tes). It was used in classical and New Testament times to illustrate the "splendor and magnificence of a visiting dignitary."

Such overwhelmingly resplendent, brilliant, noble and exalted dignitaries caused the common man or woman to fall to their faces in humble adoration.

Because Peter uses this word as he recalls his time on the mountain top with Jesus, he lets us know that this was *his own response* when he saw Jesus transfigured in all of His glory. It brought him low upon his face and prostrate before the King in humble adoration.

What a contrast this was in comparison to the behavior of the opportunist ministers! In keeping with their past record, they would have immediately snatched this as an opportunity to prove their own spiritual greatness.

Yet, it was not so with Peter. This splendid revelation of Jesus Christ in all of His glory, humbled Peter and changed his life so dramatically, that now, years later, he tells the story as though it had happened yesterday.

His life was transformed. This is the fruit of a real God-sent visitation!

The Ultimate Experience

Now Peter begins to take us step by step through this experience that he has had on the mountain top with Jesus, Moses and Elijah.

Peter says, "For he received from God the Father honour and glory, when there came such a voice to him from the excellent glory, 'This is my beloved Son in whom I am well pleased.' And this voice which came from heaven we heard, when we were with him in the holy mount" (Second Peter 1:17-18).

This was the ultimate experience! Imagine being there to observe this transfiguration of Jesus, and the appearance of Moses and Elijah standing there beside him. What an experience!

When Matthew recorded this event, he gave us the whole scenario from begining to end.

In Matthew 17:1, he tells us that this occurred "in a high mountain apart;" he tells us that "his raiment was as white as light" (verse 2); they wanted to "build a tabernacle" in honor of the occasion (verse 4); "a bright cloud overshadowed them" (verse 5); "a voice came out of the cloud" (verse 5); and "they fell on their faces" (verse 6).

This was unquestionably the highest spiritual experience possible! Any hungry Christian would have loved to have traded places with Peter, James or John that day.

In Today's Language

Look at the ingredients of this event in light of our Spirit-filled vernacular today:

— they had a "campmeeting" (verse 1).

— they saw God's glory (verse 2).

— they had an open vision (verse 3).

— they tried to start a building program (verse 4).

— they saw a "glory cloud" (verse 5).

— they heard God's audible "voice" (verse 5).

— they were "slain in the Spirit" (verse 6).

Imagine all of this happening *on one day — during one meeting!*

But Peter does not stop and stay here forever. With this fabulous and true episode still fresh in his mind, he now turns to his flock and speaks very deeply from his heart once again.

Though it would be hard to surpass the experience he had on the Mount, Peter confidently assures his readers: "We *have also a more sure word of prophecy. . . .*"

Chapter Twelve
A More Sure Word of Prophecy

After relating his fabulous story to us, Peter continues to tell us that as great as this experience was, there was something more sure and steadfast for him to build his life and faith upon.

He says, "We have also a more sure word of prophecy; whereunto ye do well that ye take heed as unto a light that shineth in a dark place, until the day dawn, and the day star arise in your hearts"(Second Peter 1:19).

It is as though Peter says, "As great as the experience on the Mount of Transfiguration was, it was fleeting and temporary. I have a word that is more sure and enduring than my experience on the mountaintop. This is a word that you can count on to be reliable forever!"

Notice that Peter calls the Word of God "a more sure word of prophecy." This was a phrase used during his day to describe the writings of the Old Testament. They were called "the prophetical word." There is no doubt that this is a reference to the scriptures of the Old Testament. Peter tells us that they are "a more sure word."

The phrase "more sure" is taken from the Greek word *bebaioteros* (be-bai-o-te-ros) and it refers to something that is "certain, stable" or "immovable." This is something which we would say is "set in concrete." It is the ultimate picture of stability and reliability.

But what is Peter comparing the written Word unto?

What is the Word "more sure" than? What is Peter's point?

By using this strong and stable word, Peter is telling us that the Word of God is far superior to any supernatural experience which man could attain, or to any contemporary prophecy that man could give.

Supernatural experiences and prophetic utterances, as wonderful and necessary as they are in our lives, come and go very quickly. They are fleeting.

This Word, on the other hand, is "immovable" and "dependable." You can count on it. As Jesus said, "Heaven and earth shall pass away, but my words shall not pass away" (Matthew 24:35).

In no way, shape or form is Peter diminishing the importance of his experience or the supernatural experiences of others. Of course not!

You must remember that in the previous verses, he has just penned his own experience for us as though it had occurred the day before. This supernatural encounter was a *major event* in Peter's life and was still *very fresh* in his mind.

Yet, as time has passed and Peter has grown in the Lord, he has learned that the "concrete, stable, dependable, reliable" scripture, is far superior to his own supernatural experience.

As I write, I think back to the personal experiences which I have personally encountered with the Lord. I have had God-inspired dreams; my ministry began on account of a visit with the Lord Jesus during a vision; and I have been transported by the Spirit to other places to share the Word of God on two different occasions. The realm of the Spirit and the supernaturalness of Jesus Christ is an integral part of my life.

These experiences were glorious and life-changing. They have made a definite and lasting impression on my life. One touch from the supernaturalness of the Holy Spirit, and one will always yearn for another. Even as I write this now, my spirit is stirred for more supernatural experiences with the

Lord. *However, you cannot build your entire spiritual foundation upon such experiences.*

Though supernatural experiences with God are wonderful, needed, and should be expected at some point in the life of every individual believer, if these are all we have to build our faith upon, we are in very desperate trouble. These experiences — which come and go very quickly — are simply not as "concrete, stable" and "reliable" as the written Word. Thus the reason that Peter calls the Word of God "a more sure word of prophecy."

In fact, Peter was so convinced that the written Word was superior to any experience, that he goes on to tell us, *". . .whereunto ye do well to take heed as unto a light that shineth in a dark place. . . ."*

A Fixation on the Word of God

Notice especially that Peter says, ". . .whereunto ye would do well to take heed as unto. . . ."

The phrase "to take heed unto" is from the Greek word *prosecho* (pros-echo), and it is a picture of a person who has a "fixation" upon something.

Prosecho is the very word Paul used in First Timothy 4:1, when he said that in the latter times some would "give heed to seducing spirits and doctrines of devils."

The word "give heed" (*prosecho*) conveys the notion of turning your thoughts toward a different direction, opening your mind to something new, or to be totally preoccupied with a thought or an object. However, the most basic idea of the word is that of a "fixation."

Because Peter uses this word in the context of this verse about the Old Testament scriptures, you could paraphrase the verse, "If you're going to be consumed and preoccupied with something, then turn your eyes and your thoughts toward the Word and develop a preoccupation and fixation upon it. If you do this, you will do well!"

How this must have shocked the Gnostic revelators of his day! Peter has enjoyed the ultimate supernatural experience available to man while on the Mount of Transfiguration, and yet, he still declares that the written Word is better, surer and more reliable — it is more trustworthy!

Again, by laying this emphasis upon the Word, he is not doing away with the vital role of supernatural experiences in the life of the Church. Rather, he is putting these experiences in their proper place of importance. In comparison to the Word, they are secondary.

God does not give these experiences in order to draw our attention away from the Word of God, nor to replace the Word of God as a substitution. Instead, He gives these experiences to confirm the Word and support what the Word has already told us.

Therefore, these kinds of experiences are secondary to the Word of God in our lives. If they were never given to us, the Word would still be enough for us!

In light of all this, Peter declares that even his own experience was secondary to the witness of scripture.

Rather than have a fixation upon this past experience — which though glorious, was fleeting — he came to discover that the "concrete, stable, reliable" and "dependable" Word was far, far superior to his own experience.

Because of it's dependability, he plainly tells us that if we are going to have a fixation upon something, then make your fixation upon this!

Real Spiritual Light

Peter continues, ". . .whereunto ye do well that ye take heed as unto *a light that shineth in a dark place. . . .*"

The words "light," "shineth," and the phrase "dark place" are extremely important in this verse about the Word of God.

156

The word "light" comes from the Greek word *luchnos* (luch-nos), and it is a reference to "a lamp"; like the lamp that sits on the table next to a sofa or recliner in a family room.

The next word, the word "shineth," is from the word *phaino* (phai-no) and is in the present active tense. The present tense indicates a "continual shining." In other words, this is not a light that shines for a few hours only; this "light shines continuously. . . ."

Then he tells the effect of this light. He says it is "a light that shineth in a dark place. . . ."

The phrase "dark place" is from the word *auchmeros* (auch-me-ros), and it refers to a place that is "dingy, dark, dreary" or "murky." It was often used to denote places that were "parched, dry" and "thirsty."

By using these words and phrases — "light," "shineth," and "a dark place" — Peter is telling us what the Word will do if we give it an important place in our lives.

This Word is like a light that knows no end; it shines, shines and keeps on continuously shining. Its brilliancy floods our murky sight and muddy perspective with clarity; and it meets the need of our parched, dry and thirsty spirit.

If it is enlightenment that we seek for, then Peter has given us *the key* to enlightenment!

Just as you would turn on a lamp on the table at the end of your sofa in order to bring more light into your room, you must reach over and pick up the Word of God and allow its light to flood your being.

You must open it, read it, give heed unto it, and allow its transforming light to shine into the dark and spiritually murky places of your life. Once this transforming light has been released into your life, every need of your parched, hungry spirit and soul will be addressed and met.

Flooded with Internal Illumination

God wants you to have light, illumination and supernatural revelation! How much does God want you to have and experience?

Peter says, ". . .whereunto ye do well that ye take heed as unto a light that shineth in a dark place, *until the day dawn, and the day star arise in your hearts."*

This scripture tells us that God's intention is for us to be so filled with the light of His Word, that we would be internally like the dawn of a new day — filled with fresh and glorious light.

Think of Peter's illustration of "the day star" or the sun. Though the blackness of night is deep, it quickly breaks up and dissipates as the sun rises and drives it out of sight.

At first, during the earliest portion of the dawn of the new day, the sun's light is dim on account of the pervading darkness. Yet, as the day passes by and the sun continues to rise, the light gets brighter, brighter and brighter — until finally, the the light shoves darkness backward — until it is removed altogether.

According to Peter, this is what God's Word will do inside of you if you permit it to have an important place in your life. This is God's will for you!

In fact, to illustrate just how much light and revelation God wants you to possess internally, when Peter refers to the "day star arising in your hearts," he uses the Greek word *phosperos* (phos -phe-ros) for the word "day star."

This word *phospheros* is a compound of the words *phos* and *pheros*. *Phos* is the Greek word "light," and *pheros* means "to carry" or "to bear." When taken together as one word, it literally means "light-bearer."

By using this vital word, Peter tells us that the Word of God is the instrument through which God "carries light" into our lives.

The word *phospheros* is where we get the term for a "phospheros light." This means God's intention is to literally flood our entire inner man with divine illumination and powerful, radiating light and revelation! As Psalm 119:130 says, "The entrance of thy Word giveth light; it giveth understanding to the simple."

True revelation and divine illumination is connected to the presence of God's indwelling Word. Peter confirms this for us again in this pivotal verse!

Setting the Record Straight

Like we are today, Peter's readers were hungry for God and His supernatural power. They would love to have an experience like the one Peter has encountered and told them about. So Peter now speaks to his flock about this important subject: *the supernatural.*

Specifically, he speaks to them about genuine prophets, how those prophets functioned, about prophecy, and about supernatural revelation.

Second Peter 1:20 tells us, "Knowing this first, that no prophecy of the scripture is of any private interpretation."

Notice that he starts out in this important verse about prophetic ministry by saying, "Knowing this first. . . ." The word "knowing" is from the word *ginoskontes* (gi-nos-kon-tes) and is a present active participle, which means this word denotes *continuous action.*

In other words, Peter is describing something that his readers must absolutely "know" right now, must "know" tomorrow, must "know" the day after that, and the day beyond that — they must never forget! *They must know it continuously.*

This alerts us to the fact that what he is preparing to say is of tremendous importance! This is so important that they must know it and never forget it!

The verse continues, "Knowing this first. . . ." The word "first" is from the Greek word *proton* (pro-ton), and it describes something that is ranked first in importance. It is this very same word that is used in Colossians 1:18 to denote the "preeminence" of Jesus Christ over all things.

Because he uses this strong word that denotes priority, importance and preeminence, he is telling us that this matter is of "tremendous importance ."

The whole idea of the word "first" (*proton*) is, "Know this first. . . ," or, "First things first!" You could even paraphrase it, "You must know this essential and foremost truth." Or even better, you could translate it, "Let's set the record straight."

And that is exactly what Peter is trying to do in this verse!

He is trying to set the record straight about supernatural occurrences and how they come to us. As he begins this *very important* section of scripture, he drives his message into the reader's heart by saying, "Know this as a matter of priority. . . first things first! *Get this straight!*"

Then he continues, ". . .no prophecy of the scripture is of any *private interpretation.*"

Private Interpretation

This phrase "private interpretation" has been greatly misunderstood by many people. However, by taking an in-depth look into the Greek, the meaning of this hard-to-understand phrase comes into clear view.

First of all, the word "private" comes from the Greek word *idios* (i-di-os), and it describes something that is "of one's own self."

Second, the word "interpretation" is from the Greek word *epilusis* (epi-lu-sis). It is a compound of two words, *epi* and *lusis*.

Epi literally means "upon," and *lusis* means "to loose, set free" or "to release." When these two words are compounded together, they describe the act of "loosing" or "releasing" something.

In light of the Greek words *idios*, which describes something that is "of one's own self," and *epilusis*, which describes a "releasing" or a "loosing," a *"private interpretation"* actually describes something that is "loosed or released from one's own self" — "at will." It really is the idea of something that is *self-projected.*

Remember, Peter says, ". . .no prophecy of the scripture is of any private interpretation. . . ."

Quite literally, this simply means no Old Testament prophet ever sat down to write prophetic utterances and scripture simply because *he decided* that he wanted to do so.

According to Peter, this would have been an impossibility. Why? Because "no prophecy. . . is of any private interpretation." This would have been something *self-projected* by the prophet — *by his own sheer will and determination* — and divine revelation, Peter says, does not come this way.

Supernatural experiences and prophetic utterances do not come forth as the result of one's own will. *These things cannot be self-projected.*

Also notice that Peter uses the word *idios* in this text. It is from this same Greek word that we derive the word *idiot*. There is an implication here that those who do attempt to loose, release, self-project or force these experiences, turn out to be rather *idiotic*.

I remember very vividly back to a time when a young man approached me in one of my meetings. He said, "I want to have a supernatural experience."

I answered him, "Well, then you must prepare your heart and stay right with God. These things are given by the Holy Ghost according to His own will." I specifically referred him to Hebrews 2:4, and attempted to explain to him that these kinds of visitations were given by God, and could not be forced.

He interrupted me and said, "I have decided that *I am going to have a God-sent vision today!* I have decided that I am going to have one, and *I am going to have it now!*"

I can remember back to when I was first filled with the Holy Spirit, I, too, wanted to experience the supernatural. In fact, my own approach was not far from the zeal I heard coming from this young brother who had approached me.

From those early days of my own experience, I learned that *you can see anything that you want to see!* If you shut your eyes tightly and bear down as hard as you can, you can even see stars and twinkling objects! But that is not the same as having a God-sent vision!

Back in those earlier times, my heart and zeal was right — but my understanding and knowledge was not correct. I thought I could force these things, and the Word clearly teaches that such experiences cannot be *self-projected* or *forced at will.*

When you study the Biblical examples of men and women who received supernatural visitations, you quickly discover that none of their experiences were self-projected or forced at will.

The Old Testament prophets and the New Testament apostles such as Paul, Peter and John, never attempted to force supernatural encounters. As a matter of fact, it was this very situation that Peter was opposing when he said, "We have not followed cunningly devised fables. . . ." Remember, the word "followed" means to "chase after, pursue or track down."

If you attempt to have a supernatural experience as a result of your own decision to have one, you are headed for spiritual trouble. If your imagination is vivid, and your spiritual desire is strong, you can see whatever your mind can imagine — and because of your great zeal, for a time you may even convince yourself that you have forced your way out into the spirit realm where you have had a supernatural experience.

Many people have attempted to do this during our day. Earlier in my experience, I attempted to do this. However, Peter says it is *not* possible to decide when you're going to have a dream, when you're going to have a vision, or when you're going to have a new supernatural type of manifestation.

This is so very important that when Peter began this text, he told us, "First things first. . . ." "Get this straight and don't ever forget it. . . ."

Why were his feelings and admonitions about this so strong? He is not negating the real supernatural manifestation of God. Absolutely not! No, no, no! Neither am I!

He is simply trying to keep his readers from entering into spiritual excess that would eventually rob them of genuine experiences which God would desire to really give them in the future .

Rather than dreaming up experiences that did not really occur, Peter admonishes his readers (and us!) to prepare ourselves like the Old Testament prophets did. The Old Testament prophets couldn't force these experiences, but they could sure prepare and sensitize their spirits for that moment when God did desire to invade their world!

While we wait on the moving of the Spirit, we must be constantly developing our spiritual sensitivity.

Setting your Sails to Catch the Wind

Pointing backward to the examples of the Old Testament prophets, Peter begins to reveal how genuine visitations do come, how we can prepare to receive them, and how we must respond once they have invaded our lives.

In Second Peter 1:21, he says, "For the prophecy came not in old time by the will of man; but holy men of God spake as they were moved by the Holy Ghost."

There it is again! Peter repeats his message once again about the nature of supernatural phenomena and prophetic utterances. He says, "For the prophecy came not in old time *by the will of man. . . ."*

This was another way of saying "these things cannot be willed, forced or self-projected." Even the Old Testament prophets, who flowed in incredible amounts of supernatural activity, could not *force* the supernatural to take place for themselves. This verse explicitly states that these things did not come "by the will of man."

Then how did it come? How did the Old Testament prophets flow in the supernatural? How do we, as New Testament believers, get in a position to move in the supernatural things of the Spirit? Does our will have anything to do with the supernatural moving of the Holy Spirit?

Peter tells us. He says, "For the prophecy came not in old time by the will of man, but holy men of God spake *as they were moved by the Holy Ghost."*

In order to better understand how the supernatural and prophetic utterances work today, notice especially the last phrase of verse 21. It says, "holy men of God spake *as they were moved by the Holy Ghost."*

In this important verse, Peter tells us how the prophets of the Old Testament functioned under the anointing of the Spirit of God. By looking at this verse, we find a beautiful illustration of the Spirit's anointing upon yielded men and women of God.

The phrase "as they were moved" is taken from the Greek word *pheromenoi* (phe-ro-me-noi).

The word *pheromenoi* was used in classical literature and in contemporary New Testament literature, to denote the action of a huge sailboat whose sails were set to catch the wind. It is used by Luke in Acts 27:15 to describe a fierce wind that caught Paul's ship and moved it along. It says, "And when the ship was caught, and could not bear up into the wind, *we let her drive. . . ."*

Once the sails of such a huge ship were raised and set,

the ship was then in a position to move if there was a wind blowing.

However, even though the sails were raised and set, the ship could not move by itself. In other words, the ship was totally dependent upon the wind. In order to move, they needed strong winds to blow against those sails and to "drive them" along.

The shipworkers' part was to prepare for sailing. By raising the sails and setting them in their proper places, when the strong winds did begin to blow, the ship was in a position to catch that wind and be driven or carried along by it.

This illustration of wind in the sails is the very picture that Peter is conveying to us concerning the nature of divine revelation, prophecy and supernatural manifestations, and how they come to us.

Genuine Prophetic Ministry

According to Peter, *genuine prophets are people who have learned how to set their sails spiritually.*

It is important to note that though the Old Testament prophet could not force supernatural activity to happen, *he could prepare himself to receive it.*

This is where our will is involved. We cannot force these experiences, but we can *decide to prepare ourselves spiritually* in the event that God would desire to pour Himself forth upon us.

God has desired to move upon the Body of Christ in a powerful manner with no results on many occasions. Why? Though He was blowing His mighty Spirit across the Church, the Church had not done her part to prepare to catch the wind of the Spirit. Therefore, when God breathed — because no preparation had been done, no one even knew that God was breathing upon him. Thus, no one, or few, moved with God.

By preparing ourselves and making ourselves spiritually sensitive, when God's Spirit does begin to move in a powerful manner, like the prophets of the Old Testament, because we have prepared ourselves and made our spirits ready, like a ship with sails that are raised and set, we will be better able to catch the wind of the Holy Spirit and be "driven along" by Him. Oh, to God that this wind would begin blowing upon us again today!

As long as the Spirit of God was moving upon the Old Testament prophet's spirit, that prophet could speak under a divine unction. However, when the wind of the Spirit ceased to blow across the sails of the prophet's own spirit, then the prophet's utterances, manifestations and supernatural activity ceased.

Like a ship with huge sails that are raised and set, he was still totally dependant upon the wind. *If there was no wind, then there was no prophetic movement.*

Preparing for Spiritual Movement

If we desire to flow in the supernatural ability of God today, we must take this example to heart and do our part to prepare to catch the wind of the Holy Spirit for our generation.

By praying, studying, fasting, seeking God and listening to His voice and repenting for sin that would clog our spiritual sensitivity, we can develop a greater spiritual sensitivity and thus set our own spiritual sails.

By making ourselves more sensitive spiritually when God does have something truly supernatural to say or do, we will be in a position to catch the wind of the Holy Spirit in our own spiritual sails and thus, be "carried along" by the Holy Spirit in a supernatural way.

Just as a huge sailboat cannot move without the wind, neither can we force spiritual movement. We are totally dependant upon the wind.

If the wind of God's Spirit is not blowing, then we cannot make anything happen. You cannot force miracles to happen by virtue of your own will; you cannot force the gifts of the Spirit to operate; you cannot force prophetic utterances at will, and so on.

Therefore, our most important task at hand is to set our sails spiritually. Then, we will be in a position to be "driven along by the Spirit of God" or "moved by the Holy Ghost."

Therefore, we must be preparing ourselves constantly. This is our responsibility!

The Prophet's Role Today

Since Peter is referring backward to the function of the Old Testament prophets, let's take a look at the word "prophet" to see exactly what it meant then, and what it still means for us today.

The word "prophet" comes from the Greek word *propheteia* (pro-phe-teia), and it is a compound of the words *pro* and *phiemi*. The word *pro* can literally be translated three ways. It can be translated: *1) "before" or "in front of," 2) "on behalf of", and 3) "in advance."*

The second part of the word "prophet" is the Greek word *phiemi,* and it literally means "to speak."

When you compound these two words, *pro* and *phiemi,* they form the word *propheteia,* or the word "prophet." This is a beautiful picture of the prophet and his prophetic role.

Together, these words tell us that a prophet is technically one who: *1) "speaks before" or "in front of" the Lord, 2) he is one who "speaks on behalf of" the Lord, and 3) he is one who "speaks in advance" of something.*

Speaking Before the Lord

"Speaking before" or "speaking in front of" the Lord is the prophet's foremost role.

Most people think of a prophet as one who stands to prophesy and to work supernatural wonders. This, however, is secondary to the prophet's primary function.

Because the word "prophet" can be translated "to speak before" or "to speak in front of," this tells us that a prophet's first and foremost task is to be "before" the Lord and to be "speaking in front of" the Lord.

This is a wonderful picture of a prophet sitting at the feet of the Lord — worshipping, adoring, listening, communing, conversing with the Lord and receiving divine direction from Him. This is that tender moment when the prophet humbles Himself before the Lord and sensitizes his heart to the Lord's will and voice.

You must remember, the prophet — like a sailboat — is totally dependent upon the wind of God's Spirit.

He cannot speak until the Spirit moves across his own spirit. To speak beforehand would be nothing more than his own human opinion — which may be good and fair — but this would not be genuine prophetic ministry.

Therefore, he sits and waits.

Sitting in the presence of the Lord and "speaking before" the Lord, he waits for the moving of God's breath upon his own human spirit.

By staying before the Lord and speaking, conversing and fellowshipping with the Lord, he is setting his spiritual sails to catch the wind of the Holy Ghost.

Once he is sensitized to the Lord's moving, and God has spoken to his heart and given him a message and the Spirit of God begins to move across his spirit, then — finally — he is in a position to turn toward the people and move into the secondary aspect of his prophetic ministry.

Speaking on Behalf of the Lord

Once the prophet has spent time "speaking before" the Lord and has clearly heard the Lord's voice for the people, then the prophet can turn to prophesy or to "speak on behalf of" the Lord.

If a prophet spends no time before the presence of God — conversing with God and listening to God — then the

prophet will have nothing to speak to the people. *His prophetic abilities are directly tied to what he has heard while he was communing with the Lord, in the Lord's presence.*

Once he knows the Lord's heart, then and only then can
the prophet turn and speak authoritatively as the Lord's rep-
resentative and spokesman.

However, because he has humbled himself and has
caught the wind of God's Spirit, when he speaks, he will
speak with a great anointing and with supernatural confirmation.

Speaking in Advance of Something

The word "prophet" (*propheteia*) also carries with it the
sense of a *predictive ability.* Thus, the reason that the word
"prophet" can be translated as one who "speaks in advance."

With the wind of God's Spirit blowing across his own
human spirit, it is not uncommon at all for a prophet to see
forward into the future.

Perhaps this is best illustrated in the New Testament by
the example of the prophet Agabus. "And in these days came
prophets from Antioch. And there stood up one of them
named Agabus, and signified by the Spirit that there should
be a dearth throughout all the world: which came to pass during the days of Claudius Caesar" (Acts 11:27-28).

Notice particularly that Agabus signified this "by the
Spirit." In other words, Agabus did not speak on his own.
This was not a self-projected prophecy. He spoke as the Spirit
of God moved upon him — under the control and influence
of the Spirit of God.

Though the genuine prophet does not function in this
"forthtelling" all the time, he or she does from time to time
move in this supernatural aspect of prophetic ministry.

Thank God for Real Prophets!

This book deals extensively with the issue of false

prophets and false teachers, because the Holy Spirit declared that this problem would emerge in the last days.

However, we must not forget to thank God for the real prophets and teachers which He has given to the Church of Jesus Christ.

These prophetic individuals and teachers have been given to the Church as a marvelous, supernatural gift to bless us and help move us forward into spiritual maturity. According to Ephesians 4:11, we cannot attain this maturity without the input of their wonderful, much needed ministries.

However, Peter's concern is not about the real prophets and teachers. His concern is about the false.

Therefore, after telling us how genuine prophets function in Second Peter 1:20-21, he immediately picks back up his subject of false prophets and false teachers once again.

Beginning in Second Peter 2:1, he gives us several additional, very important insights into how false prophets and false teachers come to exist and what will happen to them in the future if repentance does not take place.

Chapter Thirteen
Merchandising the Anointing

You must keep in mind that Peter has been speaking about real prophets in Second Peter 1:20-21. Now, he turns and begins to speak once again about the reality of false prophets and false teachers inside the Church.

In Second Peter 2:1, he says, "But there were false prophets also among the people, even as there shall be false teachers among you, who privily shall bring in damnable heresies, even denying the Lord that bought them, and bring upon themselves swift destruction."

Notice how Peter begins this verse. He says, "But there were false prophets also. . . ."

The first two words of this verse ("But there") are exceedingly important in the context of what Peter is telling us. The phrase "but there" is taken directly from the Greek phrase *de kai* (*de-kai*).

The phrase can be translated several different ways. You could translate it, "On the other hand, " or perhaps even a better translation would be, "In addition to this. . . ."

Remember, in the previous verses Peter has been speaking warmly and enthusiastically about genuine prophets. Now, by using the phrase *de kai*, Peter means to tell us, *"But, in addition to the real prophets. . . there were also false prophets."* In other words, he wants us to know that it is possible for real prophets and false prophets to co-exist.

Therefore, he says, "In addition to the real prophets which

I've just told you about, there were also false prophets. . . ."

Especially notice the phrase "there were." This phrase comes directly from the Greek word *ginomai* (gi-no-mai), and normally describes something that "occurs slowly," or "something that transpires over a period of time."

By selecting to use this specific word, the Holy Spirit is letting us know that this problem of false prophets and false teachers in the Church is not a problem that comes quickly into a place of prominence. Instead, Peter tells us that this is a phenomena that slowly develops "over the passing of time."

Jumping on the Bandwagon

What opens the door for these fraudulent ministers? Where do they come from? Who invites them to come? Why does this problem still continue to persist today?

You must know that false ministry nearly always follows several steps behind genuine ministry. You can be sure of that!

Even in Paul's ministry, he had fraudulent men who traced his steps and waited. . . They waited for him to leave a geographical area, so they could come in directly behind him with their legalistic message, and distort the gospel of grace.

In fact, if you do not take precautions against this possibility of false ministry, then you can count on it happening. For instance, if a real, God-sent prophet spends time ministering in a certain geographical area, it won't be too long until false prophets will begin gathering there too!

If a powerful teacher is in a certain vicinity, wait just a while, and you will see that it won't be too long until false teachers show up too! Likewise, if a strong apostolic brother is ministering to the church, neither will it be too long until false apostles are gathering in that area too.

Whatever God is doing at the present moment, that is what

Satan tries to duplicate. And not only this, he normally tries to duplicate these things through sincere people who have tremendous amounts of spiritual desire, and who would never deliberately want to counterfeit a gift!

There is no doubt that the majority of false ministry gifts begin very pure at heart. All of the names of the problem people which Paul mentions in his epistles had ministered with him at some prior time in his ministry. They were "right" at some earlier time.

Even Balaam, the prophet of the Old Testament who eventually tried to curse God's people for the payment of money, began his ministry as a genuine prophet of the Lord.

People are naturally attracted to whatever is the most exciting, sensational and popular thing of the hour and moment. The natural tendency of the flesh is to "jump on the bandwagon" of the latest craze, or to chase after the latest fad.

Though this is a problem of carnality which should not exist in the Church of Jesus Christ, this problem inside the Church has never been more apparent than it is now. For the past six decades, especially, people have been aimlessly running from one thing to another on a consistent basis.

For instance, during the late 1940s and 1950s, when God was restoring the fivefold ministry gift of the evangelist to the Church, it seemed that everyone "jumped on the bandwagon" and formed for themselves an "Evangelistic Association."

What a wonderful time this was in the history of the contemporary Church!

During that period, God gave the Church powerful, anointed and world-changing evangelists. These were men and women such as Billy Graham, Oral Roberts, T.L. and Daisy Osborn, Kathyrn Kuhlman, and so on. During those days, it was difficult, if not impossible, to be unaffected by these preachers and their mega-miracle ministries.

There is no doubt that during the late 40s and 50s, the evangelist was *God's emphasis* in the Church. God was truly doing a massive work to heal the sick, cast out demons, raise the dead and win millions of the lost to Christ.

Because God's hand was upon these individuals so strong, the people at large began to glamorize them and look upon them as the "mecca" of what ministry should be! This was not particularly the fault of the evangelists. This is simply the nature of flesh.

Therefore, "over the passing of time" (*ginomai*) scores of ministers, and even pastors who were enamored with the evangelistic ministry, began to leave their pastorates in order to pursue the evangelistic field!

Then came the 1960s and 1970s. During the 60s and 70s, God began to restore the fivefold ministry gift of the teacher to the Church. Since evangelists had brought millions into the Church, these converts needed teaching! Therefore, God moved supernaturally to restore the gift of the teacher.

During this period of the Charismatic Movement, tape ministries began to grow and flourish. In fact, if you actually owned a tape duplicator during this period of time, you were envied above all others! Though it sounds silly now, to own a tape duplicator nearly always meant that you were regarded very highly in a spiritual way!

God sovereignly moved and bestowed upon the Church gifted teachers such as Derek Prince, Bob Mumford, Charles Simpson, Don Basham, Ern Baxter, Charles Trombley, Kenneth Hagin and many others. These were the "big name" teachers during those days. And what wonderful teachers they were!

As a matter of fact, they were so wonderful that scores of people who had formed themselves "Evangelistic Associations" during the 40s and 50s, now began to call themselves teachers and developed for themselves "teaching ministries."

Once again, the people of God began to "jump on the bandwagon" of the hour. It wasn't long until we had piles and piles of individuals who were endeavoring to follow after the "cloud" of God's Spirit, and move over into teaching ministries.

Throughout the 1960s and clear through to the 1970s, the teacher was undoubtedly *the emphasis* that God was restoring and speaking to the Church.

Then the 1980s arrived. What an exciting period this was to be! Lo and behold, God began to restore strong prophetic voices to the Body of Christ!

God moved to speak widely through a wonderful brother, Kenneth Hagin, probably the most well-known Charismatic prophet in the nation during our time. During this period, his ministry began to grow at an unprecedented rate — and we began to become familiar with a real prophet's voice.

Brother Hagin's anointing was so strong, that now throngs of people who called themselves *evangelists* during the 40s and 50s, and then called themselves *teachers* during the 60s and 70s, were now beginning to call themselves *prophets* during the 1980s.

And what a mess this created!

Like the great evangelists of the 40s and 50s, and the tremendous teachers of the 60s and 70s, this emergence of "prophetic problem people" during the 80s, was not necessarily the fault of the real prophets which God was truly restoring to the Church at this time. This was flesh, once again, chasing after something which was exciting and sensational

And as we proceed into the 1990s, when I am confident that God will begin to restore the genuine ministry of the apostle to the Church, we will face the same dilemma again. Many people who claimed to be prophets during the 1980s, will now begin to claim that they have moved upward into the apostolic gift.

God, help us!

There's Nothing New Under the Sun

According to Peter, this is not a new problem. He plainly tells us that in the Old Testament, "In addition to the real prophets, there also — *over the passing of time* — came to be false prophets."

Imagine the problem that must have been created in Israel when God began to speak mightily through Moses! Can you imagine all the young, pure at heart and spiritually hungry, who admired Moses and wanted to be a prophet just like him!

How about during the days of Elijah, Elisha, Ezekiel, Jeremiah or Isaiah. Can you imagine the impact that these men must have had upon their nation? Yet still, can you imagine all of the people who were enamored with them and tried to duplicate their ministries?

Yet, with their strong prophetic ministries flourishing, still, the Old Testament is literally infiltrated with strong admonitions about *false prophets!*

Dear reader, if you are called to be an evangelist — then *evangelize!* You are under no obligation to teach like a teacher.

If you are called to be a teacher — then *teach!* You are under no obligation to prophesy like a prophet.

If you are called to be a prophet — then *prophesy!* There is no need for you to pretend to be an apostle.

And if you're called to be an apostle — then do the work of an *apostle!* That is what God has called you to do!

Find out what God has called you to be, and stay there! You are under *no pressure* to conform to what someone else is doing in their ministries.

The last thing the Body of Christ needs is for you to abandon your place in order to follow after another's. Not only will this create spiritual confusion in your own ministry, it will leave a vacancy behind you that was desperately needed to be filled by *you* for the Church.

But this is not a new problem.

Thus the reason that Peter looks backward to the Old

Testament. He reminds us that it has always been the habit of God's people to run from one thing to the next.

In light of this, he says, "In addition to the real prophets, over a period of time there also came to be *false prophets. . . .*"

The Great Pretenders

Peter calls these sincere, but misled individuals, "false prophets."

The term "false prophet" is taken from the Greek word *pseudoprophetes* (pseu-do-pro-phe-tes). It is a compound of the words *pseudo* and *prophetes*. *Pseudo* describes something that is "false, a sham, a hoax, a lie," or "a falsehood." The word *prophetes* is simply the Greek word for a "prophet." We covered this word in Chapter 12.

When these two words are compounded (*pseudo* and *prophetes*), you discover that by using these two words, Peter is telling us that false prophets are really "sham prophets," "counterfeit prophets," "hoax prophets," or even better, you could translate it *"pretend prophets."*

And this is the bottom line of the real problem. In the Old Testament, the New Testament, and still today, this is the bottom line problem: *sincere people, who are trying to force themselves into a gift and calling which God never extended to them.*

Though sincere and pure at heart, this always opens the door for falsehood and spiritual confusion.

Let me say it once again: Find out what God has called you to do and be, and then stay there and do it! There is no need for you to force your way into another man's or woman's calling. We do not need any more *"pretend teachers," "pretend evangelists," "pretend prophets," "pretend apostles," or "pretend pastors."*

There Shall be False Revelators

After pointing backward to this Old Testament problem

of "pretend prophets," Peter now makes his message current and up-to-date.

He says, "But there were false prophets also among the people, *even as there shall be false teachers among you. . . .*"

Recently a gentleman came to me in one of my meetings where I was teaching on this subject, and said, "Rick, you have misunderstood this text. The Bible doesn't say we are going to have a false prophet problem in the last days. It says we are going to have a *false teacher* problem in the last days."

He was correct in recognizing that Peter predicted a "false teacher" problem. Peter does say, "even as there shall be *false teachers* among you." In light of this, we must back up for a moment and take a look at this word "teacher."

The word "teacher" comes from the word didaskalos (di-das-ka-los). By the time of the New Testament and here in this verse, it was used in a rabbinical sense to convey the idea of a "revelator," or one who brings forth "new light," "instruction" or "understanding."

This means, therefore, that to a great extent (though not entirely), *the prophet and teacher fulfill the same function.* The primary difference between the two is that prophets ordinarily speak (though not always true) *by inspiration,* and the teacher gives forth revelation *by the process of reasoning and studying.*

You must understand that both the prophet and teacher "teach" to some degree. The purpose of both of these gifts is to "revelate" truth to the Church. They both stand as "revelators." Prophets differ from teachers only in that they speak *by inspiration,* and not *by reason.*

So when Peter says, "even as there shall be false teachers among you," he is lumping all "revelators" together — whether they are prophets, teachers, apostles, evangelists or pastors. All of these gifts stand as "revelators" inside the Church.

Therefore, to be technically correct, we must understand that Peter is *not* specifically predicting a *prophet* or a *teacher* problem. Rather, he is predicting a *"revelator"* problem! Any of the fivefold ministry gifts could potentially be included here.

Also notice that this problem today is simply a repeat from the Old Testament.

Just as the Old Testament saints had a *pseudoprophetes* crisis, or a *"pretend prophet"* crisis, Peter declares that we shall have a *pseudodaskalos* crisis, or a *"pretend revelators"* crisis to deal with in the last days.

Whether you call these revelators prophets or teachers, the problem is one and the same. *The issue is false revelation coming forth from people who are forcing themselves into spiritual positions which God did not give them.* Thus, I have come to call them "the great pretenders."

The Lunatic Fringe Society

As Peter continues to describe these pseudo ministers, he describes them as those "who privily shall bring in damnable heresies, even denying the Lord that bought them, and bring upon themselves swift destruction" (Second Peter 2:1).

The word "who" is one of the most important words in this verse. Because it is such a small word, it is normally missed by the casual reader. However, the Holy Spirit has chosen this word to make a very vivid, illustrative point.

The word "who" is from the Greek word *hoitines* (hoi-ti-nes). As it is used in this verse, the word *hoitines* refers to a "special class" or "category" of people. Specifically, it denotes a group of people who are so far off spiritually that they cannot fit into a normal orthodox Christianity. I call this group "The Lunatic Fringe Society."

The technical definition of the "lunatic fringe" is: "Those who make up the fantastically extreme, in order to attract and maintain an audience, and who are normally of a religious persuasion. "

They may claim to be on the "cutting edge" of a new move of God. They may purport to have new revelation that others are simply not able to hear and receive.

The truth is, this particular group (similar to the Gnostics of the early Church) is so extremely off-balance and far-out in a spiritual sense, that they simply cannot function with others. They live on the "edge" or "brink" of spiritual insanity all the time, and are so far off that they think that they are the ones who are living a normal, healthy Christian life.

In addition to this, the word "who" (*hoitines*) indicates these "outer fringe" people have a way of gravitating toward each other. In other words, "Birds of a feather still flock together."

Thank God for those brave pioneers who have truly lived on the "cutting edge" of what God is doing. However, there is a difference between the "cutting edge" and the "lunatic fringe."

Martin Luther, John Calvin, John Wesley and Charles Finney all lived on the "cutting edge" of God's work. This is where we should all want to live. We need brave men and women of God who will forge new territories for the Kingdom of God.

Again, the "lunatic fringe" is not the same as the "cutting edge."

Smuggling Gross Error Under Cover

Then Peter tells us how these extremely outlandish ministers operate. He says, "who privily shall bring in damnable heresies. . . ."

Especially notice the first part of the verse, *"privily shall bring in. . . ."*

The phrase "privily shall bring in" tells us exactly how these false revelators bring their false revelation into the Church. This is an exact description of *their mode of operation.*

The phrase "privily shall bring in" is from the Greek word *pareisago* (par-eis-ago). This word is a triple compound word that is comprised of the words *para*, *eis* and *ago*.

The word *para* means "alongside." It denotes something that is *very close* — like a *para*site. The second part of the word — the word *eis* — means "into" and it conveys the idea of "penetration." The third part of this compound is the word *ago*. It simply means "I lead."

When all three of these are compounded together, the word *pareisago* ("privily shall bring in") comes to convey the idea of "smuggling something in under cover." Literally, it describes someone who is *"leading something (ago) into* the Church *(eis) alongside (para)*. In other words, this is *covert activity*.

But what are they "smuggling" their error into the Church "alongside" of? The word *para*, because it can be translated "alongside," conveys two different ideas, both of which are correct and extremely important in this verse.

First, the word *para* indicates that these false revelators are holding their doctrine close to their side — in order to hide it or keep it under cover. The picture conveyed here is that of a person who is sneaking something into the Church without the Church knowing about it.

They realize that if they tried to introduce their false revelation right from the start, in an up-front manner, they and their false revelation would be rejected. Therefore, they keep their error "under cover" and wait for the perfect moment to introduce their deception to the saints.

By doing this, they are able to keep their *hidden agenda* under cover by first worming their way into the leadership of the Church. Then, once they have gained acceptance in the ranks, they pull their false revelation forth from under their cloke and "penetrate" *(eis)* the Church with their damnable heresies.

Second, the word *para* indicates that they deceptively

mingle truth and error alongside of each other. False revelators always lay their error right "alongside" of the truth.

By creating this mixture of truth and error — literally laying truth and error "alongside" of each other — it confuses the listener.

This is the picture of a young, believing listener, who says to himself, *"I don't know if this speaker is teaching us correctly. I've never heard anything like this before. It all sounds a little outlandish to me. I'm concerned that this man is off spiritually. . . ."*

Then minutes later, because the speaker is now mingling his error with genuine truth, the same listener speaks to himself again, and says, *"Well, I know that what he just said was right! It's obvious that this man knows correct doctrine. I guess that perhaps he is all right after all. He's just telling me some things that I've never heard. He must be on target spiritually, or he wouldn't have said what he just told us."*

Thus, by laying their error right "alongside" of the truth, their error becomes more palatable to the average listener. It is "dresssed up" in the disguise of truth.

Often these false revelators will hardly use any scripture at all in their messages. Rather, they emphasize their own spiritual escapades. Then, to make their escapades and new teachings sound acceptable to the Church, they throw in a token scripture here and there.

After one huge meeting, one such false revelator turned and said to a friend, "Did I use enough scripture to make my new revelation acceptable to the crowd tonight?"

You see, his concern wasn't the Word of God. His concern was that he has dressed up his own revelation enough to make it palatable for the people to chew and swallow.

This is especially dangerous to the new, spiritually immature, yet ready-to-learn believer. This younger believer will not have enough discernment to be able to divide the truth from the error.

If the leadership of the local church has not taken their responsibility seriously "to take heed unto the flock over which the Holy Ghost hath made them overseers" (Acts 20:28), this falsehood will most likely make deep inroads into the local assembly. When this occurs, the church has been "penetrated."

Understanding Heresies

Notice what it is that these false revelators are "smuggling" into the Church. Peter says, "who privily shall bring in *damnable heresies. . . .*"

The phrase "damnable heresies" has been tremendously misunderstood. This is not a reference to eternal damnation. Rather, this is a picture of temporal destruction in the life of a believer.

The word "damnable" is taken from the Greek word *apoleia*. It vividly describes "destruction, decay, rot" or "ruin."

The word "heresies" is from the word *hairesis* and literally means a "choice." On the basis of this alone, the phrase "damnable heresies" could be translated, "destructive choices," "rotten choices," or even "ruinous choices."

The implication of this is that we must be very careful and choosey when making spiritual decisions! However, this alone is not adequate to convey the full meaning of Peter's words.

To fully understand Peter's strong warning, we must take a deeper look into the word "heresies." We must also better understand the sentence structure of this statement in the Greek.

The word "heresies" (*hairesis*) was used in classical times to denote a "sect, group" or a "school of thought." Thus, a *hairesis* was used to denote any specific school of thought, or it was used to denote a category of similarly thinking people who had come together as an association or a group.

These different groups had specific beliefs that were

peculiar to them. They had made "choices" that had given them individuality in a crowd. In time, the word *hairesis* came to denote these people as being very *opinionated*; so opinionated, that eventually the word *hairesis* came to be associated with the word *schisma*.

The word *schisma* (schis-ma) means "division" and nearly always denotes one of those messy, divided situations that you are always hear about in some local church. For instance, these two words — *hairesis* and *schisma* — are used in First Corinthians 11:17-18, to describe a terrible division that was brewing in the church at Corinth.

In this particular case at Corinth, a *hairesis* (literally, an "opinion" or technically, a "heresy") had become so off balance and out of line spiritually, and created such a mess in the local church, that the church was now becoming divided (*schisma*) over this *hairesis*.

In Galatians 5:20, we discover that a *hairesis* ("heresy") is a "work of the flesh." Galatians 5:20 places "heresy" right in the same category of "idolatry, witchcraft, hatred, variance, wrath, strife and sedition."

Then, when you come to Titus 3:10, the word "heresy" is used once again. However, the meaning of "heresy" has taken on a new flavor by the time you come to Titus 3:10. By this time, it came to describe much more than simply an "opinionated" group or an "opinionated" person.

Now the word "heresy" came to describe — not only an "opinion" or a strong personal "choice" of belief — but it came to denote *a belief that could not be substantiated* — or perhaps even stated better, it came to denote a *subjective belief* or a *subjective experience*.

This business of basing beliefs and faith upon *subjective experiences* that could not be substantiated, was so serious, that by the time Peter wrote Second Peter 2:1, the word "heresy" came to depict a belief that was *completely incompatible* with the foundations of the Christian faith.

Spiritual Rot and Decay

As a matter of fact, these "heresies" were so incompatible with the Christian faith that Peter calls them "damnable heresies."

The Greek sentence structure is different. The Greek actually says, "heresies damnable." Or, the Greek reverses the words "heresy" and "damnable," placing the word "heresy" first, and the word "damnable" second.

Why is this important? Because Peter is telling us what heresies will produce in our lives. If you make "heresy" a part of your regular diet, then you can be sure that some kind of "damnation" will follow.

The word "damnable" (as we have already seen) describes "destruction, decay, rot" or ruin." Because of this, the whole notion of Peter's warning is this:

If all you do is sit around and eat on subjective experiences ("heresy") — *tales of angels never before mentioned in scripture, trips to heaven and beyond that contain details not recorded in God's Word, revelations that have no scriptural foundation or precedent, dreams, visions, and so on* — this will certainly not cause you to grow spiritually. Rather, if this is all you eat spiritually, then eventually this will cause you to experience spiritual "rot" and "decay."

You cannot build your life upon these kinds of experiences. Yes, absolutely, we must thank God for the genuine spiritual experiences and phenomena which do come into our lives. However, if you are one of those people who read only books about subjective experiences, you will have no solid foundation for your life when you desperately need a solid foundation.

Furthermore, if you do not change your approach to spirituality, it will not be long until you, too, become a member of "The Lunatic Fringe Society."

Living in the Grey Zone

False prophets and false teachers love to teach subjective things. The reason for this is clear: subjective experiences and teachings are difficult to prove or disprove.

For this reason, they love to live in these grey areas. As long as they stay there, they can say what they want, do what they want, and nearly teach what they want — with no accountability to the Word of God or to other leaders. They are beyond the realm of "testing."

If a man says he's been to heaven, how do you know if his story is really true or not — *unless you went to heaven with Him?*

If a special speaker says he has had a vision and has a new revelation which was given to him by an angel — how do you know if his story is really true or not — *unless you were there when the angel appeared?*

These are grey areas.

Once again, we thank the Lord for any supernatural visitation which He would give us. But we cannot — *we absolutely, emphatically cannot* — make these experiences the basis of all we preach, teach or believe, nor can we make these subjective things the diet that we constantly feed our spirits upon.

However, false revelators love to deal in these grey areas. They will stay in these areas as long as they possibly can. Why? Because as long as they are in these grey, uncontestable areas, they are able to say almost anything without having to substantiate it from the Word of God, or without having to be accountable to others.

Often these pseudo prophets and teachers stay away from the Word because they do not know it well enough to use it. On account of this, they stay away from the Word and deal only in the "spirit realm."

Peter tells us plainly that false revelators major in "damnable heresies." Or, as the Greek sentence structure says, these are "heresies damnable." In other words, a steady diet of this will produce spiritual "rot" and "decay" inside the life of a believer over a period of time.

Dr. Jekyll and Mr. Hyde

How does a genuine prophet or teacher become a false prophet or false teacher? How does this radical change occur? Is it sudden? Does it occur accidentally?

I think back to the story of Dr. Jekyll and Mr. Hyde. Dr. Jekyll, a brilliant and gifted physician, began to toy with new scientific ideas. In fact, he toyed with these ideas until they consumed him. Once consumed, he deliberately began experimentation which eventually produced the monster, Mr. Hyde. He went into his experiment — though very slowly and over a period of time — with his own full consent and knowledge.

Likewise, when you study the words of Peter in Second Peter 2:1, you discover that genuine prophets and teachers do *not* become false prophets and false teachers *accidentally*. They move over into this realm of falsehood with *full consent and full knowledge.*

In Second Peter 2:1, Peter continues, "denying the Lord that bought them, and bring upon themselves swift destruction."

Before we move to the final conclusion of this verse that forecasts the ultimate destruction of these false revelators, first we must look at the words "denying," "Lord," and the phrase "bought them." All three of these are *exceedingly important* in the context of this subject.

Though many people have used this verse as a reference to cult leaders such as Sun Myung Moon, or as a reference to unsaved preachers who deny the diety of Jesus, blood atonement or the inspiration of the Word of God, these are not the types of individuals that Peter is referring to in this verse.

Peter makes it plain that the individuals to whom he is

referring are blood purchased preachers who have "forsaken the right way, and are gone astray" (Second Peter 2:15). Thus, he depicts them as those who "deny the Lord that bought them."

The word "bought" is taken from the Greek word *agoridzo* (a-go-rid-zo), and it is one of three words in the New Testament that are translated as the word "redemption."

The word *agoridzo* is taken from the word *agora,* and by definition it describes a "marketplace." The word *agoridzo* which Peter now uses in this verse, literally means "to make a purchase in the marketplace." By the time of the New Testament, it described the act of "buying a slave at the marketplace."

By using this word, which is always associated with the idea of "redemption," it is clear that Peter is speaking of people who have been "purchased" out of bondage by the blood of Jesus; they have have been "redeemed" by Him. Because of the usage of this word, there is no doubt that these are "blood-bought" individuals.

Genuine Fivefold Ministry Gifts

Even more than this, at one time they were true fivefold ministry gifts! How do we know this? Because the verse says, "denying *the Lord* that bought them. . . ." The word "Lord" is the key here.

The word "Lord" in this verse, is not the normal word used for the word "Lord" throughout the New Testament. In fact, this particular word for "Lord" is used only ten times in the New Testament.

In Greek, it is the word *despotes* (des-po-tes). It is what we would call an administrative word. In other words, the word *despotes* ("Lord") used in this verse, would normally refer to a CEO, or a Chief Executive Officer. This is that top executive who has sole control and authority, especially over others in the executive wing.

The word *despotes* was also used to describe the Head Steward of a large household. This Head Steward had charge over all the other stewards in the house. These under-stewards reported to him, received instructions from him, were paid by him, and if the need arose, they were dismissed by him.

This word "Lord" (*despotes*) is not the word used in Romans 10:9, when Paul said, "For if you confess with your mouth that *Jesus is Lord,* and shalt believe in thine heart that God hath raised him from the dead, thou shalt be saved."

This is the word "kurios" (*ku-rios*) and it describes the general Lordship of Jesus Christ over the entire Body of Christ.

The word that Peter uses for "Lord" (*despotes*) is more *limited.* It is used *only* in reference to those who are in administration, to those who are in the executive positions, or to those who work as under-stewards and report directly to the Head Steward of a large household.

By electing to use this word, Peter is making his message clearer and clearer. Not only is he describing "blood-bought" and "redeemed" people in this verse, he is describing people who relate to Jesus in a different way from others. To them, Jesus Christ is their CEO.

These are people who have been placed into the administration department of the Church by the Lord Jesus Christ and who relate to Him — not only as their savior — but also as their Chief Executive Officer.

The word *despotes* clearly tells us that these people Peter is describing are fivefold ministry gifts, called to function as a part of the goverment of God within the Church of Jesus Christ.

Saying "No" to the Lord

Though true fivefold ministry gifts, notice what it is that they are saying to Jesus, the Head of the Church. Peter continues to tells us that they are in the habit of *"denying the Lord. . . ."*

The word "denying" is from the Greek word *arneomai* (ar-neo-mai), and it is a present middle participle. The word literally means to "deny" or to "reject."

However, because in this verse it is a present middle participle, this means Peter is painting a picture of someone who looking directly into the face of Jesus, and after hearing what Jesus has to say, turns and rejects His counsel.

The word "denying" (*arneomai*) indicates that Jesus Christ, the CEO of the Church, has spoken something vitally important to this minister. However, the minister apparently does not like the message that he has heard from the Lord. Therefore, rather than take the Lord's counsel and obeying Him, he turns his face away from heaven and rejects the counsel of the Lord Jesus Christ.

Rejecting the counsel of Jesus Christ once or twice will not make you into a false prophet or a false teacher. However, habitual rejection of the Lord's voice and the promptings of the Holy Spirit will eventually give birth to falsehood and error in any man's or woman's ministry.

The word "denying" is also important because it tells us that Jesus Christ, the Head of the Church, will not allow a ministry gift to become involved in error without first trying to correct that minister. The Lord will do everything within His power to correct a minister and bring him back into a circumspect walk. This is the nature of God's mercy.

Think of all that God did to rescue Balaam from his own destruction; even speaking through the mouth of an ass when Balaam would no longer listen to the voice of God. The Bible says Balaam "was rebuked for his iniquity: the dumb ass speaking with man's voice forbad the madness of the prophet" (Second Peter 2:16).

Yet, like Balaam rejected the counsel of the Lord, Peter says false prophets and false teachers — *though the Lord has tried to correct them and bring them back into balance* — look to Jesus, the Head Steward of God's Household, and deny His counsel; or, they tell Him, "NO!"

Reasons for Rejecting the Lord's Voice

Why the false revelators of Peter's day were rejecting the Lord's voice is not clear from this text. However, because human nature has always been the same, it is easy to make a safe assumption about these circumstances.

Perhaps the Lord spoke to the minister and said, *"I want you to stop speaking about your last supernatural encounter. Your ministry is good, but there is a wrong element in your last supernatural experience. I want you to lay it down until I show you what is wrong with it."*

Yet, according to Peter, this minister answers the Lord Jesus and says "no!"

Why? This minister may have told the Lord, *"But Lord, what do you mean? Do you actually want me to lay this teaching down? Lord, don't you understand that this new teaching is what has given me notoriety? If I lay this down, then my crowds will begin to diminish. You couldn't really mean for me to lay this down!"*

Therefore, the Lord speaks once again to the minister's heart, and says, *"Yes, I want you to lay it down."*

When confronted with obeying the Lord or losing his large crowds, this man or woman must now make a choice. According to Peter, a person with the seeds of falsehood within him, will "deny" the Lord's counsel. *"I'm sorry, Jesus, but I just can't do that. I'm not going to do what you have commanded me."*

We have all rejected the leading of the Holy Spirit at some point in our Christian experience. One, two, three, four, or maybe even 100 such rejections will not make us into false prophets and false teachers.

However, if we persist in denying His Lordship over us and make this rejection of His counsel a habitual thing in our lives and ministries, then we are opting a radical transformation of who we are in the spirit. *This is how all false prophets and false teachers get their start.*

Dear reader, pray for the leaders of the Church of Jesus Christ today. Pray that these leaders will desire to obey God more than they desire to attain the success of man. Rather than criticize, please pray. Our leaders want to obey God and they need your support through prayer.

However, should a leader turn habitually from the voice of God to go his own way, God will let him do what he wants.

The sad part of this is when that minister turns from God *habitually*, there is also a turning that takes places in his or her heart. The heart eventually becomes *so calloused* that they can no longer hear God's voice clearly, and thus, "their conscience is seared as with a hot iron" (First Timothy 4:2).

Destruction that Rips Limb from Limb

When this occurs, the Bible says that these who begun as genuine fivefold ministry gifts but who have now begun to mutate into spiritually-seared leaders, seal their own destruction.

Peter tells us that they "bring upon themselves swift destruction."

Notice three things in this verse. First, the word "bring upon," second, notice that Peter tells us this will occur "swiftly," and third, look at what these misguided revelators are going to reap: "destruction."

In the first place, Peter says, "and bring upon themselves. . . ."

The phrase "bring upon" is taken from the Greek word *epago* (ep-a-go). This word *epago* was used in other contemporary writings of that time to denote the "letting loose of wild dogs" to tear victims apart, limb from limb.

By using this graphic word, Peter is telling us that when a minister rejects the Lord's counsel and goes his own way, he is "letting loose" his own destruction.

Notice that this verse doesn't say that God will bring

swift destruction upon this person. Peter says, "and bring upon themselves swift destruction." This is a judgment which they release upon themselves. And what a terrible judgment this shall be!

Notice, too, that it doesn't take long for this judgment to take place. Peter says, "and bring upon themselves *swift destruction.*"

The word "swift" is from the word *tachinos* (tachi-nos), and it describes something that takes place "suddenly" or "quickly."

The word "destruction" is the word *apoleia* (apo-leia), and it describes "rottenness, decay" or "ruin." It is the identical word that Peter used to describe the effect of the heresy in the Church.

Because Peter repeats this word again, he tells us that what these false ministers have been sowing into the Church, is *exactly* what they are going to reap in their ministries. They are going to reap spiritual destruction, decay and rot.

The Final Straw

What is the final straw that releases this judgment? How long will God permit a man to go on masquerading like this, without allowing the natural processes of judgment to come upon him?

The story of Eli and his sons, Hophni and Phinehas, gives us a clue to these answers.

In First Samuel 2:12, we find that Eli's sons, though they were in the ministry, they did not truly know the Lord; they had no on-going relationship with Him.

They were so far from the Lord's presence, that according to First Samuel 2:14 and 22, they were actually stealing from the offerings, and were committing adultery with the women who worked in the temple. Yet, no judgment came upon them.

Their judgment was not released until they had so mistreated the people, that the people began to avoid the presence of God. This was the last straw.

It wasn't that the worshipper didn't want to come and worship the Lord; they simply didn't want to be abused by the priests when they came to the temple of the Lord to worship — and when you begin messing with worshippers, you have violated something that is very dear to God.

As the scripture says, "Wherefore, the sin of the young men was very great before the Lord: for men abhorred the offering of the Lord" (First Samuel 2:17).

God will often tolerate a backslidden preacher because he still is preaching, at least in part, the gospel. However, things radically change in the thinking of God when a minister so spurns the people, that they avoid coming to the House of the Lord in order to offer pure worship. When this happens, a minister has committed a sin that is "very great."

At some point along the way, a time and point known only to God, God removes His divine hand of protection from that minister and allows his own self-imposed destruction to come upon him.

Since Eli and his sons experienced this self-imposed destruction in one day's time, we cannot help but remember how quickly Peter said this destruction comes. He called it a "swift destruction."

A "swift destruction" is precisely what Eli, Hophni and Phinehas experienced. In one day, they were *removed*.

And not only were they removed, the entire city of Shiloh, the spiritual center of that time, which had been infested with their incorrect behavior, was wiped off the face of the earth — *never to be rebuilt again*.

Attracting a Crowd

In spite of this sealed destruction upon them and their ministries, Peter says, "And many shall follow their pernicious ways; by reason of whom the way of truth shall be evil spoken of."

Notice that Peter says, "many shall follow. . . ."

The word "many" is from the Greek phrase *hoi polloi* (hoi pol-loi), and it refers literally to "masses" or "multitudes" of people. Though many are hurt by such ministers, the Word of God teaches that they have a special knack for creating a following.

Why do their ministries attract so many? Peter continues to tell us. He says, "And many shall follow their *pernicious ways.* . . ."

Notice that it isn't really the minister that they are following, but rather it is the lifestyle and conduct of the minister that they are following. As Peter said, "many shall follow their pernicious ways. . . ."

In fact, they are so attracted to the conduct of these ministers, that Peter uses the word "follow" in this verse. The word "follow" is the Greek word *exakouloutheo* (ex-a-kou-lou-theo), and it literally means "to follow with the purpose of duplicating."

By using this word, he is informing us that the greater masses of people will love what they see these pseudo ministers do; will be attracted to it; and will even attempt to duplicate this outrageous behavior in their own personal lives.

Much of this outrageous behavior is covered in Second Peter 2:10-19. Though we will not cover these verses in this book, much of their outrageous behavior has already been covered in Chapters 5, 6 and 7.

The word "pernicious" is in Greek the word *aselgeia* (as-el-geia), and it carries the idea of "excesses."

For some strange reason, which even Peter could not figure out, it is true that the stranger a minister and his ministry is, the more people are drawn to him. No one can attract a large crowd more quickly than a spiritual flake.

As Peter said, "many shall follow their pernicious ways. . . ."

Merchandising the Anointing

He continues his graphic portrayal of them by saying, "And through covetousness shall they with feigned words make merchandise of you. . . ."

The word "covetousness" is from the often used Greek word *pleonexia* (pleo-nex-ia), and is used throughout the New Testament to denote an "insatiable greed" or a "strong desire for more, more, more and more."

In Colossians 3:5, Paul connects this word to "idolatry," and then lumps it together in the same category of the vilest of sins. He says, "Mortify therefore your members which are upon the earth; fornication, uncleanness, inordinate affection, evil concupiscence, *and covetousness, which is idolatry.*"

According to Paul, this "strong desire to have more, more, more and more," if not corrected, eventually becomes so all-consuming that he likens it to the worship of an idol. In plain language, it becomes a thing that we serve and worship.

It is also interesting that when Peter wrote about "covetousness" in this verse, he wrote in the locative tense. This tells us that false prophets and false teachers function *totally* from a greedy vantage point. In fact, they are "locked in a sphere of greed" and do everything they do with one thing in mind: *how will this help profit me!*

By looking at the word *pleonexia*, we discover what it is that these false revelators are primarily after. The word *pleonexia* ("covetousness") is primarily used in Greek literature to denote "an insatiable desire" for 1) *more money,* 2) *more power,* or 3) *more influence.*

Peter tells us that this is the realm from which these error-ridden ministers function. They desire more cash, more personal power, and greater influence over others.

An Insatiable Desire for Money

There is nothing wrong with money, power or influence as long as it is held in balance under the Lordship of Jesus Christ.

Everyone needs money!

You must have money to pay your bills, to purchase your food, to make your house payment, to pay for the fuel in your car, to pay your taxes, and so on. It is impossible to live in our world today without money.

In the same way you must have money to pay your personal bills, ministries also need money to pay their ministry expenses.

They need money to pay the salaries of the people who work for the ministry, they need money to pay electricity bills, phone bills, printing bills, tape duplicating bills, office supplies, and so on.

Then after these are paid, they must have money to fulfill the outreaches which God has put on their hearts.

To do this, they need money for missions, evangelistic crusades, free materials for prisoners, free materials for missionaries overseas, radio bills, television bills, production bills, book printing bills, etc. None of this is cheap, and the world doesn't give it to you! It is all very, very expensive.

However, we must not become so consumed with our need for money, that it becomes an idol in our lives or ministries. *In order to avoid this pitfall, we must stay before the presence of the Lord and keep our motives pure.*

If we do not make it a priority to stay before the Lord and to keep our hearts pure in regard to the issue of money, it will not be long until our "need for money" develops into a "love of money." First Timothy 6:10, plainly tells us that it is this "love of money" which is "the root of all evil."

Notice that Paul did not say that *money itself* was evil; but rather, the *love of it* was evil.

The "love of money" in a ministry will eventually stain

the gospel ministry and the gospel message with disgrace. The "love of money" is a powerful force which Satan uses to distort good ministries into spiritual perversions — and when this happens, it nearly always brings embarrassment upon the Body of Christ.

This is the reason that Paul said, "which while some coveted after, they have erred from the faith, and pierced themselves through with many sorrows" (First Timothy 6:10).

Notice he says, "they have erred from the faith. . . ."

Why would "covetousness" cause a spiritual leader to "err from the faith?"

Because in time, if money is the bottom line and driving motive of a man's or woman's ministry, though he or she may have started out humble, pure in heart, as a valid ministry with a good message for the Body of Christ, they will do *whatever is necessary* to bring in money.

This is when preachers and ministries revert to fund raising tactics that are intolerable for a man or woman of God.

They may try to dress their tactics up to look spiritual. This, however, is nothing more than a disguise — perhaps to convince themselves that what they are doing is all right, or perhaps to convince others that what they are doing is all right.

Paul referred to these kinds of tactics in First Thessalonians 2:5, where he states that he absolutely *refuses* to behave in this manner. He says, "For neither at any time used we flattering words, as ye know, nor a cloke of covetousness; God is witness."

Notice that Paul associates "covetousness" with "flattering words."

The idea of "flattering words" is giving flattery to others for the sake of selfish interests. This is a person who tries to win people over, not because he loves people, but because he loves what the people have and own — and wants it for himself. This is deception for selfish ends. *This is spiriutal maniuplation.*

Paul also tells us that these types of individuals are very slick operators. They are so smooth in their deceptive tactics that they have learned to cover up their greed in a "cloke of covetousness."

The word "cloke" is from the Greek word *prophasis* (pro-pha-sis), and it depicts a "pretense."

This is the notion of putting on an appearance in order to impress someone or to make a gain of them financially. The word "cloke" actually conveys the idea of changing colors, changing styles or patterns if necessary to obtain what you want. This is nothing more than an outward show to meet the selfish interests of the actor.

When Paul bid the Ephesian elders farewell in Acts 20:33, he proudly told them, "I have coveted no man's silver, or gold, or apparel."

These tactics may work for the world's best advertising agencies, but we are not the world. *Though some of these avenues of fund raising may raise large amounts of funds, they erode our spiritual influence — and no amount of money is worth eroding our spiritual influence.*

Don't be confused about the issue here. The real issue isn't whether or not ministries use advertising agencies. It may be that God *would* direct a ministry to use such talented people to better reach people. There is nothing inherently wrong with this.

The real issue is, "What is our true motive for ministry?" "Are we acting in response to Christ's call to reach and help people, or are we simply attempting to help ourselves?"

Peter tells us that false ministers, especially, are not able to keep this financial area in balance in their ministries.

To let us know how motivated these fraudulent ministers are for money, he uses the word "covetousness" to describe their activities. In plain language, this means they minister to make money, and not to help people.

Once again, churches and ministries need money in

order to fulfill God's call to reach the world for Jesus Christ. However, this "need for money" must never become a "love of money."

An Insatiable Desire for Power

Neither can we allow the desire for "power" to overtake us.

By "power" I mean to refer to an abnormal desire to promote one's self above others. This is a deception which Satan has used to destroy many men and women of God throughout history.

I cannot help but to think of King Saul. When the call of God first came to Saul, he said, "Am I not a Benjamite, of the smallest of the tribes of Israel? And my family the least of all the families of the tribe of Benjamin? Wherefore speakest thou to me?" (First Samuel 9:21).

From the content of this verse, it is clear that when God first called Saul, he was small in his own eyes. Yet, as time passed by, Saul's perspective of himself began to dramatically change. In fact, it changed so drastically that it eventually cost him his kingship and the kingdom.

As Samuel pronounced God's judgment upon King Saul, he sorrowfully said to him, "When thou wast little in thine own sight, wast thou not the head of the tribes of Israel, and the Lord anointed thee king over Israel?" (First Samuel 15:17)

Samuel's statement, "when thou wast little in thine own eyes," is a key to Saul's backslidden and fallen condition.

Something changed and turned sour inside Saul after he had tasted the privilege of human power and authority. Though once "small" in his own eyes, now he saw himself as "big" in his own eyes. This inner change was so massive, that he lost sight altogether of his accountability to God, and even obviously felt he could disobey God without consequences.

Once elevated by God into leading positions, many men and women of God have allowed the taste of "power" to spoil them. And according to Peter, false prophets and false teachers thrive on this thrill of "power."

We must never forget that the apostle John warned us, "For all that is of the world, the lust of the flesh, and the lust of the eyes, and the pride of life, is not of the Father, but is of the world" (First John 2:16).

An Insatiable Desire for Influence

The word "covetousness" also pertains to our third point: *an insatiable desire to have influence and control over people.*

This abnormal desire for control over people is exactly what the apostle John was referring to in Third John, verses 9, when he said, "I wrote unto the church: but Diotrephes, who loveth to have the preeminence among them, receiveth us not."

He goes on to say, "Wherefore, if I come, I will remember his deeds which he doeth, prating against us with malicious words: and not content therewith, neither doth he himself receive the brethren, and forbiddeth them that they would, and casteth them out of the church" (Third John, verse 10).

What was it that John said this troublemaker named "Diotrephes" wanted? Like all false ministers ultimately desire, he wanted to possess "the preeminence" among the brethren.

The word "preeminence" is from the word *philoproteuo* (phi-lo-pro-teu-o) and is a compound of the words *philos* (phi-los) and *proton* (pro-ton). *Philos* means "love" and conveys the idea of an "infatuation," and *proton* simply means "first" or "the first place."

When taken together as one word, the word "preeminence" (*philoproteuo*) describes a person who is "infatuated and preoccupied with his own sense of self-importance." It denotes the mindset of a person who is "deeply in love with the idea of holding a high-ranking position above others."

This desire to lord themselves over others is a common

trait among false prophets and false teachers. Please understand that if you know someone with this trait in their life, this does not necessarily mean that they are a false minister. However, you can be certain that if this flaw is not corrected, in time it will lead this minister to commit *spiritual manipulation.*

On account of the fact that these particular ministers are obsessed with the idea of controlling the lives of other people, they have actually entered into a type of *spiritual witchcraft.*

What do I mean by "witchcraft?" Witchcraft technically concerns itself with "manipulating and controlling situations."

It is clear from John's words that Diotrephes' felt his "preeiminent" position in the Church was threatened by the arrival of John and his companions.

Realizing the spotlight could shift from him to John, he began to act immediately, and in a vicious way, to erradicate John's credibililty. Thus, he became a classic, typical "spiritual manipulator." This was spiritual witchcraft of the highest order.

John tells us, "and not content therewith, neither doth he himself receive the brethren, and forbiddeth them that they would, and casteth them out of the church" (verse 10).

Like other deceivers, it is clear that Diotrephes was "threatened" by the presence of John, and therefore, he threatened his own followers with rejection.

Though we cannot be certain of his exact conversation with his followers or of the message that he preached to them, it appears that he must have declared something like this: *"If you receive the apostle John or any of his companions, I will personally have you thrown out of this fellowship! I forbid you to have anything to do with him. You are my disciples and no one else's."*

Diotrephes reverted to carnal tactics in order to control the lives and thoughts of others. When leaders like Diotrephes are abnormally driven to possess influence over others, this is truly an act of genuine "covetousness."

For some reason that is unknown to us, this kind of person gets his sense of self-importance by controlling others. Therefore, when their followers are drawn to someone else's ministry or simply expresses an interest in someone else's ministry, this poses a great threat to the false minister.

If this "threat" is not removed or alleviated, then the spiritually manipulating leader may revert to the same kind of lying and slanderous tactics that Diotrephes used in order to eradicate John's influence.

All three of these things, *1) an insatiable greed for money, 2) an insatiable greed for power, and 3) an insatiable greed for influence*, are carried over to us in the word "covetousness."

As you well see, these are serious marks of a fraudulent minister. Peter wants his readers (and us!) to be aware of these marks and develop a sense of discernment about these critical characteristics of falsehood.

Prophecies that Benefit the Prophet

Peter continues, "And through covetousness shall they with *feigned words* make merchandise of you."

The phrase "feigned words" is also very important in this text. It is taken from the Greek word *plastos* (plas-tos), which is where we get the word "plastic."

Originally, the word *plastos* was used to illustrate the act of moulding clay or wax into a specific shape. It was also used to describe the act of "forgery"; like a forged piece of artwork, a forged signature, or a counterfeit dollar bill.

The very fact that this word can be translated "forgery" tells us that these individuals are not innocent in their behavior.

It is impossible to "forge" an art masterpiece without knowing that you are doing it. It is impossible to "forge" another person's signature without knowing that you are violating their rights and wronging them. Likewise, it is impossible to accidentally "forge" a dollar bill. If a person carries out a "forgery," he or she is clearly doing it *with full intent to deceive.*

Because Peter uses this word (*plastos*), he is unmistakably telling us that false ministers willfully "forge" words from the Lord, prophecies, teachings, etc., in order to deceive and make some kind of financial gain from the saints. This is absolutely clarified since Peter continues to tell us that the real intention of these frauds is to "make merchandise" of the Church.

Because the word *plastos* also describes the act of moulding clay or wax into the shape that the potter desires, this gives us another clue to the way false ministers operate.

Just as a potter has power over his clay or wax, and can mould it into any shape that pleases him personally, the false prophet and false teacher moulds his words to benefit himself; as would profit *him* the most.

All serious scholars agree that this phrase "feigned words" refers to insincere prophetic utterances that benefit the prophet financially, with no real regard for the need of the people. This is a picture of a person "making up" words at will. If possible, these "made up" words will somehow coax the listener to respond in a financial way.

What these individuals are prophesying is emphatically clear. Peter has already told us that they operate in the sphere of "covetousness." Now, by paying heed to the phrase that follows, we discover again that pseudo ministers have money on the mind. He tells us, "with feigned words shall they make merchandise of you. . . ."

Therefore, it is clear from the context of this verse that "feigned words" and "forged prophecies" specifically have to do with *prophetic utterances that manipulate money out of your pocket, and into theirs.*

Peter could not have selected a stronger word to make his point. Like plastic that that can be bent and twisted, these pseudo prophets and phony teachers bend and twist their teachings and utterances to benefit themselves above all others.

Spiritual Merchandisers

Peter continues the verse by saying, "with feigned words shall they *make merchandise of you. . . ."*

The word "merchandise" in this verse bothered me personally for many years. Why? Because my own ministry makes tape series, books and other teaching materials available to people who desire to obtain them.

On account of this, I was particularly aware that "merchandising" the Word of God was wrong and was something we needed to stay away from. In light of my concern, I began to study the word "merchandising," and after research, I found that this word has to do more with the idea *wrong motives* than it actually does with selling.

The word "merchandising" is from the Greek word *emporeomai* (em-po-reo-mai), and it was to describe the act of "trading, trafficking" or "selling" in the marketplace.

However, there is more to this word than this! The word *emporeomai* was used technically to denote wandering con artists who set up a tents in marketplaces, and then *deliberately sold flawed merchandise to buyers* who thought they were purchasing something of fine quality.

Because of the deception of these sellers, the word *emporeomai* came to depict the unethical behavior of these fraudulent merchandisers.

After these wandering merchants "felt out" the crowd in each new marketplace, and then determined what kind of merchandise they could sell the most of to that particular crowd, then they turned to their traveling trunks and pulled out the products they knew would appeal most to this new group.

Peter's message here is straightforward and plain. What is he telling us?

He is telling us that false ministers are not genuinely

committed to any specific portion of God's Word. Instead, they are committed only to the section of scripture that is going to excite the crowd the most that night, and that is going to put the most money in their pockets when the offering is taken at the end of the service.

Sleeping Before Judgment Falls

In spite of the fact that these deceiving ministers have blatantly abused the Church of Jesus Christ and continue to do so, Peter tells us that they are numb to the reality of judgment.

The verse says, "whose judgment now of a long time lingereth not, and their damnation slumbereth not" (Second Peter 2:3).

This verse can be divided into two sections. First, he speaks of a judgment that "lingereth not." Second, he warns us that their "damnation slumbereth not."

The phrase "lingereth not" is from the Greek phrase *ouk argei* (ouk ar-gei) and is in the present active indicative tense. This means that the judgment spoken of in this verse is not sitting "idle."

Rather, the phrase *ouk argei* indicates that even as Peter writes these words, *this judgment is awake, strong and vigilant, and is at this very moment marching forward at full speed to execute the sentence that has been pronouned upon these deceivers.*

However, these deceivers have been deliberately abusing God and His people for such a long period of time, that they have become numb to the serious nature of their sin.

By ignoring the Holy Spirit's pleading to stop their wrong activities, they have seared their consciences so that they can no longer hear what the Spirit is attempting to say to them.

However, though they may be sleeping in the face of the reality of their soon coming judgment, Peter tells us that their "damnation slumbereth not."

The word "slumbereth" (*nustadzei*) is used only one other time in the New Testament besides here. It is used in Matthew 25:5, when Jesus relates the story of the five foolish virgins to His disciples.

In this parable, Jesus told of five wise virgins who realized the soon coming of their bridegroom, and therefore, immediately begin to make preparations for his arrival by trimming their lamps and filling them with precious oil.

On the other hand, there were five foolish virgins, who though they knew their bridegroom was coming, wrongly thought they had a long period of time to prepare for his arrival.

Because they were negligent of the hour and wrongly thought they had a long time to prepare for his coming, they went to bed and "slumbered" while the other five wise virgins vigorously trimmed and filled their lamps with oil.

When the bridegroom suddenly arrived, the five foolish, neglectful virgins awakened out of their sleep to discover they had waited too late to make their preparations. When they cried out for mercy and admitted their folly, they learned that their fate had been sealed. The bridegroom answered them, "Verily I say unto you, I know you not" (Matthew 25:12).

Jesus concluded this parable, saying, "Watch therefore, for ye know neither the day nor hour wherein the Son of Man cometh" (Matthew 25:13).

Because Peter uses the same word "slumber" that is used in Matthew 25:5 about the five foolish virgins, he is implicating that like the foolish virgins did not realize the seriousness of the hour, so also false prophets and false teachers do not realize how quickly judgment will come knocking at their door.

While they may be asleep to the harsh thought of judgment, the Bible says their damnation is not sleeping. They may ignore this reality for as long as they wish. However, "out of sight, out of mind" will not work in this case.

Whether they are awake to the soon coming arrival of their own destruction or not, this will not hamper or thwart the judgment that has been released and is now moving forward in their direction.

Chapter Fourteen
Compassion That Reaches Into The Fires Of Judgment

Up until this point, we have primarily dealt with the problem of false prophets and false teachers and how to recognize them.

We have studied what the Bible says about their character flaws, their unfounded visitations and revelations; we have observed their fruit, what their teaching is like, and we have seen Peter's vivid description of how they carry on and operate in their public ministries.

Now we must move beyond this "identification mode" and see what the Bible says about our personal responsibility concerning this issue.

Therefore, we must ask, "What is our personal responsibility when we see a good ministry begin to take on the characteristics of falsehood?"

What is our role? Are we to judge? Are we to ignore it? Should we just forgive and forget it? Should we pray? *What are we supposed to do?*

Recent decades have brought us face to face with some of these difficult issues, whether we wanted to be confronted with them or not. We all have had opportunity to observe good ministries deteriorate into *public embarrassments* for the Body of Christ.

Perhaps there is nothing more heart-rending than to watch a good ministry begin to take on the characteristics of falsehood. It is saddening to observe them as they make serious judgment errors about their ministries and themselves, and thus lay their ministerial ethics and morals on the line.

Once we know what the Bible teaches about such things, *then we must pray for a way to help correct the problem.*

We must turn our attention to resolving the dilemma; we must see how we can help restore some of these leaders back into vital, functioning roles once again within the Body of Christ.

Though some have "forsaken the right way, and have gone astray," we must remember that the gifts and calling of God are still "without repentance" (Romans 11:29).

Therefore, we must make intercession for these who have made ethical and spiritual judgment errors. We must earnestly pray that "they may recover themselves out of the snare of the devil, who are taken captive by him at his will" (Second Timothy 2:26).

The Fires of Judgment

Before we continue studying what Peter has to say about judgment, first we must return to Jude's epistle for a moment. Though divine judgment is unavoidable for fraudulent and unrepentant leaders, Jude emphatically urges us to do all we can to rescue these leaders before this judgment occurs.

Just as he previously urged us to "earnestly contend for the faith," now he urges us to action once again by saying, "And of some have compassion, making a difference: and others save with fear, pulling them out of the fire; hating even the garment spotted by the flesh" (Jude 22-23).

Jude 22-23 can be segmented into five important points:

First, we must carefully examine the word "compassion" to see what all it entails. Second, what does the phrase "making a difference" mean? Third, what does Jude mean when he tells us, "others save with fear?" Fourth, what is the "fire" that Jude alludes to in this verse? Fifth, we must understand the phrase, "hating the garment spotted by the flesh."

Compassion for the Spiritually Sick

First, Jude says, "And of some have *compassion*. . . ."

The fact that Jude would use the word "compassion" tells us that Jude is not vengeful toward these sinister ministers. Quite the contrary! The word "compassion" rather indicates that he was extremely concerned about their spiritual well-being.

So sick and diseased were these bogus prophets and phony teachers, that he couldn't help but have pity for them; but pity *alone* wasn't going to remedy the deep-rooted problems of these deceived leaders. The remedy could only *begin* with the feelings of this human emotion.

The word "compassion" is taken from the Greek word *eleao* (e-lea-o), and it refers to the deep-seated and unsettling emotions a person feels when he has seen or heard something that is terribly sad.

These are the kinds of emotions that well up inside when you see a child whose stomach is bloated from malnutrition and who is starving. . . These are the emotions you feel when you see a man who is emaciated and is dying of terminal cancer. . . Or when you see a family who is so destitute that they are forced to live on the streets with no food and no money.

Jude's purpose in using this emotional word is very plain. He is doing exactly what television programs do when they flash pictures of starving children with bloated stomachs on the television screen in front of you. The pictures which the producers of these programs have chosen to show us are the worst scenario pictures that stir us to *action*.

After flashing these miserable pictures from Third World countries in front of us, with moving, emotional music being played as a background, then comes the call for action. The celebrity host on the program says in an impassioned voice,

"Pick up your phone and call today. . . Your call could save the life of a child."

These kinds of television programs are designed to stir up emotional feelings of "pity." Because we are so mentally busy today, to simply state the need verbally would never get our attention. Therefore, these programs make the need as graphic as they possibly can, knowing that pictures speak a thousand words; and knowing that these photos will arouse "pity" from our hearts.

However, arousing "pity" is not the ultimate goal of these kinds of programs. These horrifying pictures and emotional musical backgrounds are designed to get you to pick up your phone, call the operator's number of the television screen, and make a donation to help their cause.

This compulsion to *act* and to *do something* to help is where "pity" becomes "compassion."

Pity, by itself, would simply feel sorry about the situation. Compassion, on the other hand, cannot sit by and watch the scenario grow worse. *Compassion reaches out to act immediately and to do something about the situation.*

It is unmistakably clear that Jude wants to elicit an emotional response from his readers. He wants them to graphically see and understand how destitute false prophets and false teachers really are. He wants his readers to "feel" for these critically ill spiritual patients.

In fact, he wants them to "feel" their condition so badly, that he says, *"And of some have compassion. . . ."* In other words, take that "pity" and turn it into action!

The word "compassion" (*eleao*) depicts a person who is compelled to action because of something that he has heard or seen. In other words, when genuine "compassion" begins to flow from your heart, you *cannot* sit idly by and simply "feel sorry" about a situation.

Rather, real "compassion" says, *"Let's get up and do something about this!"* It immediately begins to seek an avenue for change and deliverance for the afflicted person.

This kind of compassion is a mighty force that reaches out even into the flames of judgment and destruction; it is so strong that it fears no enemy, and is restrained by no demonic boundaries or human limitations.

In his epistle, Jude has been very fierce, straightforward and hard on this issue of false prophets and false teachers.

He has rightfully been hard on them because of their damaging fruit within the life of the Church. However, because he knows a grim judgment awaits them, mercy floods his being as he now urges his readers (and us!) to have "compassion" on these spiritually sick people.

This doesn't mean you have to ignore what they have done; neither does it mean that you must endorse their incorrect behavior. But real compassion cannot just shut it's eyes to the problem and wait for judgment to come — *real compassion must reach out to do something about the problem. It cannot leave the deceived leader in his deceived condition.*

Because Jude uses the word "compassion" in this verse, the spiritual implication of this is that *the plight of a deceived leader is just as real and miserable as that of a starving child, a dying man, or of a destitute family.*

Your hostility toward these erring ministries will not set them free. This being the case, why not allow the love of God to build up within you until you can accurately see the reality of their spiritually ill condition.

If you allow this love to permeate you, it won't be long until genuine compassion begins to replace any feelings of hostility that you have had for that individual. With this divine flow in operation you will begin to see things more clearly.

When your thoughts are cleared of anger and animosity, then an accurate picture of this will come into focus in your mind. Rather than holding onto the feelings of anger and animosity toward these deceived people, you will be *compelled* to see them set free from their bondage. *That compulsion is the activity of compassion!*

Would you harbor anger at a child for starving? Of course not. Would you hold hostility in your heart toward a terminally ill patient for being sick? Of course not. Would you have contempt for a family that was going through difficult economic times? Certainly not!

You may think, "Yes, but these false prophets and false teachers have gotten themselves into their own mess! Why should I have compassion on them?"

Would you have compassion on a homosexual who had contracted AIDS? Didn't he get himself into his own mess? Yet, when you see his or her wasting body and helplessness, doesn't it still grab hold of something in your heart and make you wish there was a cure for AIDS?

Though it is true that most false prophets and false teachers have become false by choice, we cannot shut up the bowels of God's compassion within us. These deceived leaders need a touch of God's power more now than ever before.

You must not allow the enemy to sow wrong attitudes in your heart toward any person who has ministered under the pretense of falsehood. These are spiritually ill and desperate individuals. According to Jude, their plight is just as serious and life-threatening as any of these other terrible conditions which we have seen.

Yes. . . it is absolutely true that they have hurt many people with their damnable teachings and false revelations.

Yes. . . it is absolutely true that they have abused the Church of Jesus Christ.

Yet, harboring anger toward them does not remedy their spiritually diseased condition, and neither does it produce the fruit of the Spirit in you.

Let the supernatural compassion of Christ begin to flow out of your heart toward these people, even if you think, *"What good is my compassion? They don't even know who I am?"*

It doesn't matter that they are personally unaware of you. Compassion is a mighty spiritual force that releases incredible amounts of power. By releasing a flow of this power toward these error-ridden leaders, you, dear friend, could set in motion the very deliverance these individuals sorely need from the powers of darkness that bind their souls and deceive them.

Deceived leaders are spiritually ill; they have somehow developed a terminal, spiritual sickness. They may be so off-base spiritually that they may not even realize that they have now become mad "dogs" (Philippians 3:2) and "grievous wolves" (Acts 20:29). To a certain degree, because of deception, they could be *innocent* in their activities.

Therefore, they need a divine touch from God that will open their eyes and will bring them out of this bondage; they need healing. In fact, their spiritually ill condition is so severe that they may never recover *unless* there is a divine intervention by God on their behalf.

This is why Jude urges us to release this delivering flow of compassion. He says, "and of some have *compassion. . . .*"

Spiritually Disabled Individuals

After covering this first point in Jude's admonition, then we come to the second point: "And of some have compassion, *making a difference. . . .*"

The phrase "making a difference" is taken from the Greek word *diakrinos* (dia-kri-nos), which is a compound of the words *dia* (dia) and *krino* (kri-no). The word *dia* primarily carries the idea of "penetration," and *krino* means "to judge" or "to determine."

When the two words are compounded into one word, they depict a person who is "thoroughly unstable" and who is "unable to reach a conclusive, definite and enduring decision." This mental instability has "penetrated" his entire being; it is throughout.

Jesus used the word *diakrinos* in Mark 11:23 to describe "doubt." He said, "For verily I say unto you, That whosoever shall say unto this mountain, Be thou removed, and be thou cast into the sea; and shall not *doubt* in his heart, but shall believe that those things which he saith shall come to pass; he shall have whatsoever he saith."

The word "doubt" from Mark 11:23, and the phrase "making a difference" from Jude 22, are both taken from the word *diakrinos*. In Mark 11:23 the word *diakrinos* describes an individual whose instability is so chronic, that it is translated as the word "doubt." It is the graphic picture of an individual who cannot decide anything for himself. In James 1:8, James called this type of person "double-minded."

By electing to use this word, Jude tells us the deceived people he has been discussing in his letter are *extremely unstable;* they are unable to come to concrete conclusions for their own spiritual lives — not to mention their incapability to come to rational spiritual conclusions for the spiritual lives of other people.

The reason for this gross instability is pointed out to us by Paul in Second Timothy 2:25, where Paul tells Timothy how to help and correct spiritual troublemakers. He says, "In meekness *instructing* those that oppose themselves. . . ."

Rickety Foundations and Shaky Conclusions

The word "instructing" is a major key to understanding this problem of false prophets and false teachers.

The word "instructing" is taken from the Greek word *paideuo* (pai-deu-o), and it was used to illustrate "the training, education" and "instruction of a young, immature child."

Originally the word *paideuo* referred to the act of enrolling a young child in his first classes at school where he would learn how to behave with other children, and where he would get the very basic instruction that he needed before he went on to higher levels of education.

216

Because Paul uses this word in reference to *false revelators* and *spiritual troublemakers,* he is painting a picture for us which gives us the foremost reason why these now suppposedly mature individuals cannot come to sensible spiritual conclusions. He lets us know why they are so spiritually unstable and off-base.

Because the word "instruct" (*paideuo*) refers to the basic education and training of a young child, the implicaton is that these off-base prophets and teachers somehow missed spiritual kindergarten, and thereby have failed to learn the basics they needed before being promoted to higher levels of understanding.

In other words, these misguided individuals were never taught the foundational ABC's of the Word of God; they have skipped spiritual grade school and now are trying to deal in mature matters without having a solid foundation behind them.

For instance, the preacher (Chapter Seven) who urged people to stay away from pastors and leaders who were unduly heavy on their emphasis of the Word of God, obviously missed spiritual kindergarten. These kinds of outrageously wrong statements reflect that this person was promoted too fast, without first being grounded in basic spiritual things.

Paul makes it very clear that the reason such misguided prophets and teachers are so extremely off-base is because of their lack of foundational teaching before they became well-recognized. They never received the basic training, education and instruction in the Word of God which they needed.

Therefore, since they have no foundational teaching as a part of their own spiritual foundation, it is no small wonder that these off-base leaders have come to *illogical spiritual conclusions about spiritual things.*

Just imagine the mess that would be created if a child never went to school, never learned his ABC's, never learned how to spell, etc., and yet he still aspired to become a leading physicist.

With no rules of science in his background, no understanding of the universe, no knowledge of chemistry, and barely able to spell his own name, this poor child would be bound to make drastic errors and mistakes.

Regardless of how sincere his desire was to be a physicist, and regardless of great his desire was to do a good job, he would be unqualified for this kind of job. Though sincere, most of his scientific conclusions would be thoroughly wrong and inconclusive.

This is the very image that Paul has in mind when he tells Timothy, "In meekness *instructing* those that oppose themselves. . . ."

Furthermore, the word *paideuo* ("instructing") indicates that in order for Timothy to correct the doctrinal problems of these troublemakers, he must sit down with these deceived people, look them directly in the face and begin to teach them the basic ABC's of God's Word that they were never taught before.

The problem is, by this time pride has entered into the picture. It is very rare that a well-known, recognized, error-ridden minister is humble enough to sit down and receive instruction in the basics from someone else. By this time, they almost always purport to be "beyond" this basic type of instruction.

The truth is that if they had received a good, solid foundation in the Word of God when they were still young believers, they wouldn't be making the drastic spiritual mistakes that they are making right now. As it stands, their horrifying doctrinal miscalculations are evidence that they missed their ABC's.

Though sincerely desirous to be used by God, these misguided spiritual leaders to whom Paul is referring simply do not have the sound Biblical foundation they need in order to reach solid, stable, and reliable spiritual conclusions.

Because they do not have a foundation on which to

stand, they are "thoroughly unstable" in regard to spiritual things.

They are tossed to and fro, here and there, and are constantly chasing after one thing, and then another. Since they have no firm foundation on which to build their spiritual convictions, they are attracted to every new teaching and doctrine that blows through the Church.

This chronic spiritual instability is corrected only one way: *by going back to the foundation and learning the basics of God's Word!* According to Hebrews 5:14, it is this basic knowledge of God's Word that gives the ability to discern between right and wrong.

This is the very reason that Paul told Timothy to "instruct" them. It is as though Paul tells Timothy, *"Take the boys to school and give them some education!"*

Therefore, when Jude declares, "And of some have compassion, *making a difference,"* he is referring to the *illogical spiritual conclusions* of error-ridden ministers.

Again, the phrase "making a difference" (*diakrinos*) has to do with one's inability to come to a final, stable, reliable conclusion about a matter. It is very obvious from this that *people get into spiritual error because they are uninstructed in the truth.*

In spite of all that Jude has said in his epistle about false prophets and false teachers, by using this word *diakrinos,* he is actually giving them the benefit of a doubt regarding their motives, behavior and activities.

Rather than accusing them of doing *deliberate harm* to the Church through their damnable teachings, he basically says, *"Bless their hearts! They obviously never received a good, solid foundation for their spiritual lives. No wonder they can't come to logical spiritual conclusions, they don't even know their ABC's."*

This is the very reason that these misguided leaders need the help of compassion.

There's No Time to Lose

Jude continues to make this third point: *"And others save with fear. . . ."* (verse 23).

The word "save" is from the Greek word *sozo* (pronounded sod-zo), and in this verse it is used in the present active imperative tense, which means the Greek calls for immediate, fast and continuous action. Furthermore, this is not a suggestion from Jude; this is a *command.*

The word "fear" is from the word *phobos* (pho-bos), and it refers to a "fear" that results from a threatening or alarming circumstance. The fact that Jude would use this word indicates that these error-ridden ministers were on the brink of some type of destruction.

This is the very reason that Jude's readers are commanded to act fast and immediately. These deceived leaders are on the edge of imminent disaster. If someone does not act fast on their behalf and do what they can to save them, they *will* suffer destruction.

Therefore, Jude commands his readers to move to action *right now!* Because the circumstances are so serious, they must do everything within their power to "save" these individuals as quickly as possible.

Compassion that Reaches into the Flames

Then Jude gives us his fourth important point: *"pulling them out of the fire. . . ."*

As we proceed in this verse, Jude's visual image of judgment is becoming clearer and clearer. Because Jude is a parallel book to Second Peter, and because they cover much of the same material, it is evident that Jude, like Peter does in his epistle (Second Peter 2:6-9), has before him the image of Lot escaping from Sodom and Gomorrah just before the fires of judgment fell.

Lot was literally "snatched" out of this raging holocaust by two angels whom God had sent there to destroy the city.

As you shall see in the pages to come, Lot was so backslidden and spiritually calloused, that he did not want to leave the condemned city, even when he knew judgment was coming. The angels had to literally "snatch" him out of the city before the fire fell.

In light of this example of Lot, Jude alerts us to our responsibility to help deceived people. If their conscience is seared like Lot's was, they may not realize how deceived they are or how serious their spiritual condition really is. Therefore, we must obey Jude's command and take upon ourselves the same role that the angels assumed on behalf of Lot. We must "pull them out of the fire. . . . "

The word "pulling" is from the Greek word *harpadzo* (har-pad-zo), and it conveys the picture of "snatching" someone (like Lot and his family) out of a dangerous situation. It would be better translated "to seize."

The very fact that Jude would use the word *harpadzo* indicates that some individuals will have to be *forcibly removed* from their spiritually dangerous position; just as the angels took Lot by the hand and forcibly made him leave Sodom and Gomorrah.

In fact, when you study the story of Lot's departure from Sodom and Gomorrah, it appears that Lot's conscience was so terribly seared, that the angels had to literally take him by the hand and "drag" him out of the city against his will (Genesis 19:16).

Likewise, we must do everything within our power to "snatch" people from their spiritually dangerous predicaments. Though they may not feel the heat of the fire at the moment, or though they may not realize the seriousness of their spiritual conditon, they will experience a judgment of some kind if we do not intervene on their behalf.

Therefore, rather than sit idly by and watch them be consumed, we must reach out to see them delivered from the judgment they are about to bring upon themselves.

The primary way of reaching out to them is the subject of the last chapter of this book.

When Hate is Right

For Jude's fifth point, he says: *"hating even the garment spotted by the flesh."*

The word "hate" which Jude uses in this verse, is taken from the word *miseo* (mis-eo). It is the very word which Jesus uses when He speaks to the church of Ephesus and Pergamos in Revelations 2:6 and 2:15 about the damnable teachings of the Nicolaitans. In both instances, Jesus says He "hates" the deeds of the Nicolaitans.

The word "hate" is one of the strongest words in the Greek language. It is so volatile that it carries the idea of "violence." So when Jude tells us to "hate" the garment spotted by the flesh, he is actually telling us that we should exercise spiritual violence toward this type of *fleshly contamination.*

And notice specifically *what* part of the garment has been contaminated. Jude says, "hating even *the garment. . . ."*

The word "garment" used in this verse, refers to a person's "undergarment," and not to the outer robe that a person wore in the public. Why would Jude use this odd word?

This tells us that the *moral contamination* that Jude is concerned about, is a contamination that has gone beyond a mere surface contamination, and has now begun to even contaminate the deepest part of this person's being.

In other words, the filth Jude alludes to is not merely a surface, superficial, outward problem; like the superficial, outer cloak of a person's clothing. Rather, this filth symbolizes a moral deficiency that touches the deepest, hidden parts of an individual.

The implication is that this defilement began as an outward problem, like loose soil on the outer robe of a man's clothing. However, because this superficial dirt was never washed away, it has now began to permeate the material and rub all the way through to the undergarments.

According to Jude, these hidden parts have been *"spotted."* The Greek word for "spotted" is the word *spilos* (spi-los), which means to "stain, defile" or to "contaminate." It is from here that we get the word "spill."

In other words, this is a person who at first only had a superficial problem, but now has become *thoroughly defiled.* This defilement is so rank, that it has spread throughout his entire being. It has "spilled" into every area of his or her life.

If we do not act on their behalf, they will experience the terrible effects of this error as they begin to reap what they have sown. Therefore, realizing the seriousness of this foul condition, Jude says, "And of some have compassion, making a difference: others save with fear, pulling them out of the fire; hating even the garment spotted by the flesh."

Sinning Angels, The Flood of Noah and Sodom and Gomorrah

When you study what Peter has to say about these things, he says that false prophets and false teachers are so spiritually contaminated that they "slumber" to the reality of divine judgment.

While they know that a judgment may await them on account of their activities, they live like the five foolish virgins (Matthew 25:1-13) who made no preparations for the bridegroom's soon coming; not realizing the seriousness of the hour or how very soon judgment will arrive at their door.

The continuous, unrepentant behavior of false prophets and false teachers indicates that they have coaxed themselves into believing that they will somehow escape the trauma of judgment. How could they think this?

In the first place, you must remember that they have continued their fraudulent actitivities for so long, that now their consciences are seared. Because their conscience has become calloused to the tender dealings of the Holy Spirit, it is probable that they can no longer "feel" conviction of sin when the Holy Spirit does attempt to convict them.

Having lost touch with the critical nature of their sin, and no longer feeling any sense of remorse for what they are doing, they likewise have lost touch with the reality of punishment for their erroneous behavior.

Perhaps they have deceived themselves to believe that when it comes down to the final hour of judgment, God's mercy will overrule the sentence they deserve — and therefore, He will forgive them, shut His eyes to the pain they have caused for others and will not hold them accountable for their actions.

This, dear friend, is a deception.

Peter says that if God declared judgment upon angels who sinned; and if God destroyed the world of Noah's day because of their ungodliness; and if God refused to ignore the sin of Sodom and Gomorrah, and thus destroyed it with a holocaust; then why would He now ignore the activities of these individuals who blatantly disobey Him?

Just as He judged angels and the world of Noah's day, and as certainly as He held Sodom and Gomorrah accountable for their deeds, you can be certain that God will hold these false prophets and false teachers accountable for how they have behaved inside the Church of Jesus Christ.

Peter says, "For if God spared not the angels that sinned, but cast them down to hell; and delivered them into chains of darkness, to be reserved unto judgment; and spared not the old world, but saved Noah, the eighth person, a preacher of righteousness, bringing in the flood upon the world of the ungodly; and turning the cities of Sodom and Gomorrah into ashes condemned them with an overthrow, making them an example unto those that after should live ungodly" (Second Peter 2:4-6).

Judgment Passed on Sinning Angels

In order to make the point that God is not a respecter of persons, Peter points backward to Old Testament examples of divine judgment.

He begins his first example by using the illustration of judgment that befell the angels who sinned. Peter says, "For if God spared not the angels that sinned, but cast them down to hell; and delivered them into chains of darkness, to be reserved unto judgment" (Second Peter 2:4).

Notice how Peter begins this verse. He says, *"For if God spared not. . . ."*

Right from the start of this verse, Peter tries to awaken the "slumbering" false prophets and false teachers to the steadfastness of God's justice. It is as though Peter says, *"Do you think you are more special than angels? If God spared not the angels, then where is your justification to believe that you will escape accountability to God?"*

It is very interesting to note that Peter says, "For if God spared not. . . ." The word "spared" is taken from the Greek word *pheidomai* (phei-do-mai), which simply means "to spare."

The reason that this is so interesting is because this is the very word which Paul used in Acts 20:29, when he described the unmerciful behavior of false prophets and false teachers. He said, "For I know this, that after my departing shall grievous wolves enter in among you, not *sparing* the flock."

Therefore, in the same way that false prophets and false teachers have shown no mercy to the flock of God and have abused them, the Bible says that God *"spared not"* the angels who sinned. In other words, God held nothing back when he dealt with these sinning angels. He gave them the full sentence that their crime demanded.

You must keep in mind that Peter is simply using this illustration of sinning angels to make his point that God will judge all equally. Inherent in this passage is a solemn warning that neither will God make allowances for any supposed, special spiritual leader. If He will judge angels, then you can be sure He will judge us as well.

This is another classic case of "whatsoever a man soweth, that shall he also reap" (Galatians 6:7). Because these "grievous wolves" of the New Testament did not spare the flock of God, neither will God spare them when the time of His judgment draws nigh. Since they have sown destruction, they will also reap destruction.

Peter continues, "For if God spared not *the angels who sinned. . . .*"

There has been a tremendous debate over the years as to who these particular groups of angels are. Some have speculated that this is a reference to the fallen angels who had sexual relations with women in Genesis 6:2, thus producing a short-lived generation of half-demon, half-human beings.

It would seem that the Bible and extra-Biblical Jewish literature would confirm that this is the case. However, the problem arises in the fact that there is no definite article before the word "angels" in the Greek.

Therefore, this lack of a definite article seems to indicate that Peter is making a broad, sweeping statement about God's dealings with angels in general. Rather than translating it, "For if God spared not *the* angels," it would be better translated, "For if God spared not *angels. . . .*"

In other words, Peter's emphasis is not upon *which* angels were judged, but rather, his emphasis is upon the fact that *even* angels were judged. However, it is probable that these were the sinning angels who took women unto themselves in Genesis 6:2.

Notice what God did with this particular class of sinning angels. Peter says, "but cast them down to hell; and delivered them into chains of darkness, to be reserved unto judgment."

What a horrible judgment to be pronounced upon angels.

The word "hell" is taken from the Greek word *tartaros* (tar-ta-ros), which was originally a pagan word used in classical mythology to describe an underground cavern where rebellious spirits were assigned to reside until the time of judgment.

By using this special word, Peter tells us that these particular angels who sinned have certainly not escaped divine retribution. Rather, God has *"cast them down into hell. . . ."* Or perhaps a better translation would be, God has "cast them down into *a place of detention. . . ."* Why would this be a better translation? Because *tartaros* was just that; a place of detention; a holding tank for rebellious spirits.

Peter continues, "For if God spared not angels that sinned, but cast them down into hell; *and delivered them into chains of darkness. . . ."*

Now Peter covers three very important points about God's judgment upon these angels. First, he lets us know that God *personally* delivered these angels into *tartaros*. Second, Peter tells us that God *personally* bound them in chains. Third, he tells us that this detention place called *tartaros* is a place of black, black darkness.

For Peter's first point, he tells us that God personally *"delivered them. . . ."*

The word "delivered" is taken from the Greek word *paradidomi* (pa-ra-di-do-mi), and it refers to the act of "handing something over to someone else, to deliver something to someone for their safe keeping" or "to commit to another."

The picture here is extremely graphic and dramatic. This is actually the picture of God Himself reaching over to pick these rebellious angels up by the back of their necks, and then personally placing them into *tartaros,* a place of detention, for their safe keeping until a later time when they will be permanently judged.

The implication is the sin of these angels was so great and terrible, that God could not ask other angelic beings to execute this judgment for Him. He had to execute this judgment *personally.* Therefore, God Himself *personally apprehended* these angelic offenders and set them in a place where they would be forever restricted.

In the second place, notice what their condition was like once they were delivered by God into this holding tank called *tartaros.* The Word says that God "delivered them *into chains. . . .*"

The picture is getting more and more graphic. We discover that not only did God personally hand them over into this place of detention, but he also personally bound them in "chains."

Imagine the horror that one would experience if he knew that God Himself was going to assign him to a place of detention, and that God was going to personally bind him with supernatural chains that could not be broken. Yet, this is *exactly* what God did with the angels who sinned.

However, there is actually more to the word "chains" than first meets the eye. Though it is absolutely true that God did place the angels in "chains," the word "chains" which Peter uses *does not* really refer to "chains."

The word translated "chains" comes from the Greek word *siros* (si-ros), which was used to describe "underground pits" which served as granaries for crops. It is from this ancient word that farmers have obtained the name *silo* for the huge granaries that holds their crops today.

However, the earlier meaning of the word *siros* was that of a "dungeon, pit, or cavern." It was this word that Peter used when he said that God "delivered them into *chains. . . .*"

In light of this, this verse would be more correctly translated, *"and delivered them into dungeons, pits and caverns. . . ."*

This idea of a "dungeon, pit or cavern" is in perfect agreement with the theological idea of *tartaros* — that fallen angelic detention center which is a subterranean abyss where ungodly immortal spirits are sent until the time of the Great White Throne Judgment.

If this is the case, then why does the King James Version of the Bible translate the word *siros* ("dungeons, pits or caverns") incorrectly as the word "chains?"

Because when Jude made reference to this very same judgment upon sinning angels to which Peter is making allusions to, he used a very similar Greek word to describe their residence in *tartaros*. Jude used the word *seira* (sei-ra), which is closely connected to the word *siros*. The word *seira*, used by Jude, *does* refer to real "chains."

So the great theological debate over the years has been: "Did God place them in dungeons, pits and caverns, or did God place them in chains?" The answer is clearly that God did *both* of these things. God delivered them into dungeons, pits and caverns, and God personally bound them with supernatural, unbreakable chains.

Then Peter tells us what this subterranean detention center is like! He says, "and delivered them into chains *of darkness. . . .*"

The word "darkness" is from the Greek word *zophos* (zo-phos). It describes "blackness, blackness, blackness." One expositor has called this, "dense blackness, forever darkness," or "a place mute of all light." Another has called this "the gloom of the nether world."

There is no doubt that this would be the ultimate judgment to be pronounced upon an angelic creature. These angelic creatures had originally been created to live in the light of God's glory. To bind them in supernatural, unbreakable chains, and to place them in dungeons that are "forever black" would be the ultimate judgment for an angel.

And notice how long they are to be kept in this *"forever darkness."* Peter says, *"to be reserved unto judgment. . . ."*

The word "reserved" is the Greek word *tereo* (te-reo), and it is used in this verse as a present participle. This means these angels are literally *"being continually kept, guarded and held in continuous, unending reserve. . . ."*

It is very interesting to note that the Epocryphal Book of Enoch records God's dealings with the fallen angels who had sexual relations with women in Genesis 6:2. In respect to these fallen angelic creatures, Enoch 10:4 says, "Bind Azazel (a demon) hand and foot, and place him in darkness. . . ." The Epocryphal book of Baruch also records these dealings. Baruch 56:13 says these fallen angels were to be "tormented in chains" forever.

Regardless of the validity of these Epocryphal citations, it is clear from Peter's text that God truly *"spared not the angels that sinned."*

The Flood of Noah

Now Peter moves beyond the example of the sinning angels, to his second illustration of God's steadfast judgment.

He says, "And spared not the old world, but saved Noah the eighth person, a preacher of righteousness, bringing in the flood upon the world of the ungodly. . . ."

Notice that Peter begins this second example the same way he started his first illustration. He says, *"And spared not. . . . "*

Once again, it is as though Peter says, "If God spared not the angels, and if God spared not the world of Noah's day, then who are you to think that He would make a special exception for you?"

The verse says that God "spared not *the old world. . . ."*

Notice especially the words "old" and "world." The word "old" is from the world *archaios* (ar-chai-os), and it describes something that is "ancient." The word "world" is from the word *kosmos* (kos-mos), and it literally describes the "ordered world." In other words, the word *kosmos* doesn't refer to the natural world, but to "ordered things" in the world — like civilization, culture and society.

Why is this important?

Because once again, Peter is telling us that God is no respecter of persons; neither is He a respecter of civilizations. His justice is so steadfast, that when the world of Noah's day continued unrepentantly in their sinful ways, he completely destroyed that entire "ancient civilization." Literally, *He wiped it out!*

Only eight people from that early, ancient civilization survived the flood which God brought upon the world. This is why Peter continues to say, *"and saved Noah the eighth person. . . ."*

The word "saved" is from the Greek word *phulasso* (phu-las-so), and it means "to save, protect, preserve" or "to guard." What a powerful message this is to us!

Though the judgment of God may fall upon the world around us, God will "save, protect, preserve" and "guard" those who belong to Him. Notice also that Noah was not the only person whom God guarded during the deluge. Noah was the "eighth person." Quite literally, this refers to the fact that there were seven others with him in the Ark at the time of the flood. One expositor has even translated this verse, "and saved Noah, one of eight people. . . ."

While Noah and his family were resting safety in the protection and care of God's hands, look what happened to the ungodly world of that time. The Word says, *"bringing in the flood upon the world of the ungodly. . . ."*

The phrase "bringing in" is from the old word *epago* (ep-a-go). We saw this word used earlier in Peter's letter, back in Second Peter 2:1, where Peter depicts the judgment that false prophets and false teachers "bring upon themselves."

As before, the word *epago* was first used to denote the letting loose of wild, vicious dogs upon a victim. These dogs were so ferocious that they literally ripped the victim to pieces, limb from limb.

Now Peter uses this same word to illustrate what the flood did to this "ancient civilization." The flood, like a ferociously wild dog, took that "old world" and tore it to pieces, until finally there was nothing at all left from that ancient civilization. *God wiped it out!*

This devastation was so complete that when Peter described the flood, he used the Greek word *kataklusmos* (ka-ta-klus-mos), which means "to innundate, flood, overwhelm," or "to submerge with water." It is from here that we get the term for a "cataclysmic event."

This was a cataclysmic event which God brought upon *"the world of the ungodly. . . ."* The word "ungodly" is from the Greek word *asebes* (a-se-bes), and it is a description of those who live "outrageously sinful lives."

It did not matter to God that this flood would wipe out all historical records of that early society; or that it would destroy all of man's progress up until that time. The continuous, unrepentant behavior of that "ancient civilization" demanded the steadfast justice of God.

There is no doubt that God remained faithful to His own righteous standard and *"spared not the old world. . . ."*

Sodom and Gomorrah

Finally, Peter comes to his last and most dramatic example of God's steadfast judgment. He brings us to the illustration of Sodom and Gomorrah.

Peter declares, "And turning the cities of Sodom and Gomorrah into ashes condemned them with an overthrow, making them an example unto those that should after live ungodly. . . ."

First of all, notice that Peter says, *"and turning the cities of Sodom and Gomorrah to ashes. . . ."*

The Greek sentence structure is different from the King James Version. The Greek actually says, "and turning into ashes the cities of Sodom and Gomorrah."

To accurately understand how terrible the destruction of Sodom and Gomorrah really was, we must look at the Greek word for the phrase *"turning into ashes"* in order to grasp the full picture that Peter is giving us.

The phrase "turning into ashes" is taken from the Greek word *tephroo* (te-phro-o), and it literally means "to reduce to ashes." In this particular verse, it could also be translated "to cover with ashes."

It is interesting to note that this is the very same word that the Roman historian, Dio Cassius, used to describe the volcanic activity of Mount Vesuvius. This provides an even greater insight to the divine retribution that came upon the cities of Sodom and Gomorrah.

According to Dio Cassius, the inner rim of the volcanic ridge of Mount Vesuvius was constantly growing brittle. From time to time, this extremely brittle ridge would collapse and come crashing down into the deep throat of the huge volcano. Eventually, the entire top of the mountain collapsed. After this, it wasn't long until that collapsed portion settled and became completely concave.

In light of the way that Dio Cassius used the word *tephroo*, new images are painted for us concerning the fire that fell on Sodom and Gomorrah.

It appears that the plains of Sodom and Gomorrah were burned so badly and were so extremely brittle because of the holocaust that fell upon them, that not only were they covered with ash, eventually this brittle geographic area collapsed — until there was not even a minor hint left of these huge, major metropolitan cities.

This is the reason that Peter says goes on to tell us that God *"condemned them with an overthrow. . . ."*

The word "condemned" is taken from the word *katakrino* (ka-ta-kri-no), and it is a compound of the word *kata* (ka-ta) and *krino* (kri-no). *Kata* literally means "down" and the word *krino* is Greek word which means "judgment" or "sentence."

Because Peter compounds these two words together, the implication is that this judgment was self-imposed by Sodom and Gomorrah. Their own unrepentant ways is what released this severe judgment down upon themselves.

This divine retribution was so severe that Peter uses the word "overthrow" to describe what happened to these cities. The word "overthrow" is from the Greek word *katastrophe* (ka-ta-stro-phe), and you have probably guessed it; this is where we get the word *catastrophe*.

Therefore, this was a "catastrophic event" that occurred to the cities of Sodom and Gomorrah. In fact, it was so catastrophic that when it was all said and done, there was absolutely nothing left of these areas but smoke. The Bible says that when Abraham got up the next morning after Sodom and Gomorrah's destruction, when he looked toward the cities all that he could see was "smoke."

"And he looked toward Sodom and Gomorrah, and toward all the land of the plain, and beheld, and lo, the smoke of the country went up as the smoke of a furnace" (Genesis 19:28).

A Sculptor's Small Scale Model

Peter continues, "making them *an example* unto them that after should live ungoldy. . . ."

This is a warning which we must heed!

The word "example" is taken from the world of the artist. It is from the word *hupodeigma* (hu-po-deig-ma), which was first used to describe "a sculptor's small scale model" of a statue or monument.

Before the sculptor makes the larger, finished product, first he experiments on a small scale model. On this small scale model, he meticulously works to make certain each measurement and dimension is correct. Finally, when his small scale is proportionally exact and has met his stiff artistic requirements, then he takes that small scale model and amplifies it into the real, final product.

This, according to Peter, is what Sodom and Gomorrah

was: *it was like a scupltor's small scale model!*

So when Peter says that God made Sodom and Gomorrah an "example unto those that after should live ungodly," he is telling us in the plainest and clearest of words, that Sodom and Gomorrah was just a *prototype* of the judgment that will come in the future. *It was just a small scale model of the real judgment which is still yet to come!*

By taking this example to heart, it becomes clear once again that God's justice has always been steadfast in the past, and it will continue to be steadfast in the future!

How This Applies to You

Remember that Peter began this text by talking about false prophets and false teachers who were "slumbering" to the reality of divine judgment.

Through the verses which we have studied in this chapter, we have discovered that Peter has repeatedly said to us, "If God will judge angels, and if God would destroy the entire world of Noah's day with a flood because of their wickedness, and if God would reduce the cities of Sodom and Gomorrah to ashes because of their rebellion, then where is your rational justification to believe God would not be steadfast in His justice toward false prophets and false teachers today?"

Therefore, in light of this reality which Peter has driven into our hearts, as we come to the close of this chapter we must ask ourselves the following important questions:

"What can we practically do to help rescue false prophets and false teachers from their own destruction?"

"What role does God want us to take in order to see these leaders who were once pure in heart set free from the deception that binds them?"

"In what practical, everyday ways can I be used as a vehicle of compassion that will set in motion the deliverance that these false prophets and false teachers desperately need?"

In the next and final chapter of this book, we will see how the Lord will use you to deliver the godly out of temptation. God's merciful desire is to stop the natural processes of judgment with a divine intervention.

You are a major part of this supernatural intervention of God on their behalf.

Chapter Fifteen
The Lord Knows How To Deliver The Godly Out of Temptation

Before we discuss how we can practically help to resolve the deceived condition of false prophets and false teachers, we must look at the *specific example* of deception that Peter gave us to illustrate this problem.

Look who was living in the middle of Sodom and Gomorrah before the fires of judgment fell: Abraham's nephew, Lot!

What in the world was a man like Lot doing in a place like this? Furthermore, why would Peter use Lot to illustrate the deceived condition of false prophets and false teachers in this chapter?

Lot is a perfect example of everything Peter has been discussing in Second Peter 2:1-6. Lot was a genuine man of faith who fell into sin and deception.

It wasn't that Lot was ignorant about the dangers of sin; he simply ignored and tolerated sin until the sinful environment of Sodom and Gomorrah wore down his resistance; he made critical judgment errors about himself and his family; and thus, he laid his morals on the line and it eventually cost him his wife and his children.

By using Lot as an example in the context of a chapter about false prophets and false teachers, Peter is giving us additional insights about falsehood in the ministry. One thing is for sure, we know that Lot started out as a real man of God.

Knowing this, it is evident that Peter wants us to know that the majority of false prophets and false teachers, similarly to Lot, start out as genuine men and women of faith.

Somewhere along the way, these misguided individuals have fallen into the wrong crowd and have become influenced by the wrong people. In fact, as you will see from the life of Lot, it is this wrong influence that has assisted in leading false prophets and false teachers down the road to spiritual corruption and moral depravity.

For a moment, let's look back at the life of Lot and see what we can gain from his story.

Lot was adopted by Abraham at a young age when his father (and Abraham's brother), Haran, died prematurely. Having been adopted by Abraham after his father's death, he had grown up in the same household with his famous uncle and aunt, Abraham and Sarah, who had never been able to produce children of their own.

Lot was there the day Abraham suddenly came home, anxiously summoned the family together, and told them that God had spoken to him in an audible voice. As a matter of fact, on that same day Lot heard the gospel of Jesus Christ, thousands of years before Jesus was ever born. The scriptures teach that God had personally preached the gospel to Abraham on that day (Galatians 3:8).

He watched as his wealthy uncle took his first steps of faith. He personally observed the difficult process Abraham and Sarah experienced as they obeyed their new God and separated themselves from their former occultic and idolatrous worship of the moon. He watched as they sacrificed their luxurious home in Mesopotamia in order to pursue the voice of God.

Lot was with Abraham and Sarah when they started their faith journey, and actually took those first steps of faith along with them as the entire family journeyed beyond their homeland of Ur of the Chaldees, in pursuit of "a city whose builder and maker was God" (Hebrews 11:10).

He sat in the crowd and listened as his uncle preached about a promised city, whose builder and maker was God. Though the location of this city was unknown and it made no natural sense, he watched throngs of people pack up their belongings and mount on traveling beasts, in order to follow Abraham out of the city of Haran in pursuit of this unknown place.

Lot was with Abraham when they passsed through Sichem, unto the plain of Moreh. He saw the Cannanites and the giants that were in the promised land; he helped build the altar on which they offered burnt offerings to the Lord; he saw God's supernatural protection which was on them while they briefly sojourned in Egypt.

Lot was not ignorant or naive about the things of God! He personally partcipated in the adventures of faith which we read about today, and which we teach to others. In fact, we have even heralded these adventures of faith as the example of faith which we must seek to duplicate in our own lives.

Because Lot personally participated in this "faith walk," *you can be absolutely certain that Lot was a man of faith just like his uncle, Abraham!*

Yet, with all of this marvelous experience with God behind him, he deteriorated into a man with a mind that was nearly *reprobate.*

Though he had seen God move, and though he had walked the "walk of faith" with his famous uncle, he gave in to the evil influence around him in Sodom and Gomorrah and became morally and spiritually corrupt.

In spite of his sad end, Lot was not deceived at the first. Rather, he was a genuine man of faith in those earlier days. He had seen God move in supernatural ways and he knew God personally for himself.

Yet. . . when the opportunity arose, this "man of faith" made his home in the midst of the world's most wicked cities, Sodom and Gomorrah.

239

How Does Spiritual Deterioration Begin?

Lot's moral deterioration, as often is the case wih false prophets and false teachers, began very *slowly.*

Abraham and Lot were so blessed with an abundance of flocks, herds and tents, that it became physically impossible for one parcel of land to support both of their residences simutaneously.

Genesis 13:6-7 says, "And the land was not able to bear them, that they might dwell together: for their substance was great, so that they could not dwell together. And there was a strife between the herdsmen of Abram's cattle and the herdsmen of Lot's cattle. . . ."

In light of this space problem, Abraham made this suggestion: "Let there be no strife, I pray thee, between me and thee, and between my herdsmen and thy herdsmen; for we be brethren. Is not the whole land before thee? Separate thyself, I pray thee, from me: if thou wilt take the left hand, then I will go to the right; for if thou depart to the right hand, then I will go to the left" (Genesis 13:8-9).

The Bible says, "And Lot lifted up his eyes and beheld all the plain of the Jordan, that it was well watered every where, before the Lord destroyed Sodom and Gomorrah, even as in the garden of the Lord. . . . Then Lot chose him all the plain of the Jordan; and Lot journeyed east: *and they separated themselves one from the other. . . . And Lot dwelled in the cities of the plain, and pitched his tent toward Sodom.* But the men of Sodom were wicked and sinners before the Lord exceedingly" (Genesis 13:10-13).

Several significant insights to the deterioration of Lot can be pointed out from these verses.

First, it must be pointed out that Lot's moral and spiritual deterioration did not begin until he and Abraham *"separated themselves one from the other."* As long as Lot was still under Abraham's strong spiritual influence, he did well.

It was when *"they separated themselves one from the other"* that serious character flaws began to manifest in Lot's life. This is when he *"pitched his tent toward Sodom."*

The implication is Lot was not nearly as strong as people had thought him to be. All along, his great spiritual strength had been drawn from Abraham. Therefore, when Abraham, his spiritual mentor, was out of the picture, Lot's spiritual strength waned and his resistance to temptation came crashing down.

Keep in mind that Peter is using Lot as an illustration in the context of false prophets and false teachers.

By using this illustration, he is telling us that just as Lot was not spiritually equipped to handle life on his own, many people who are genuinely called into the ministry are sent forth on their own before they are spiritually mature enough to handle the temptations that go along with public life.

It may appear that they are strong and stable; Lot appeared to be strong and stable too. Unfortunately, many stories can be told about young men and women who started out right in their ministries, but once removed from the strong, stable influence of their spiritual mentors they got off into some type of error that revealed they were never as stable as they were previously thought to be.

All the character flaws and immaturity that had never been dealt with in Lot's life, began to surface once removed from Abraham.

These were not new character flaws; these were flaws that had always been tucked away and hidden somewhere within the personality of Lot. *He always had the capacity to do these things.*

The new situation didn't create these flaws, it simply released them. Prior to this time, Abraham's influence in Lot's life had restricted these works of the flesh. But with Abraham out of the picture, the blemishes which were always present but hidden, began to find expression.

Many parents have been shocked to discover new sides

to the personalities of their children. Through high school their child never got into trouble, always obeyed his parents and made excellent grades. Their child was the perfect example of obedience.

However, once at college an unexpected change often occurs. That spotless record from high school becomes a distant memory from the past as the same child now becomes involved with sin, drunkenness, debauchery, and fails miserably in respect to his or her grades.

What created this change? Was it something in this new environment? Is something wrong with the school? *What has created this monster?*

The truth is that the monster was potentially there all along; it had simply been restricted by the influence and supervision of the young person's parents. A couple of more years and additional experience with God would have nailed these flaws permanently to the cross.

Likewise, by sending a young preacher out too fast before God has time to deal with the hidden flaws in his or her life, can often plunge them into the depths of self-deception.

The new public place of ministry doesn't create the flaws; it simply creates an environment where those flaws that have always been present can begin to rise to the top (i.e., arrogance, pride, deception, etc.) In other words, this person always had the capacity to do these things.

In connection with this, it must also be pointed out that Sodom and Gomorrah was culturally very similar to Ur of the Chaldees. Ur of the Chaldees was a place overtaken with idolatry and rank sensuality.

Memories of the past and hidden flaws beneath the level of Lot's flesh immediately drew him close to the comfortable environment of sin that he had grown up with in Mesopotamia.

It was because of these hidden, never-dealt-with flaws,

that the Bible says Lot *"pitched his tent toward Sodom. . . ."*

Lot did not immediately barge into Sodom in order to participate in it's sin. Rather, he "pitched his tent toward Sodom," or he slowly began to direct his thoughts toward the activities of the cities. *His imagination begin to delve into things that a man of God shouldn't entertain.*

This is a picture of mentally playing with sin. Though he didn't go there in person at first, *he went there mentally.*

Play with sin long enough in our mind, and eventually those thoughts will control you, drag you out, and entice you into actual participation.

From the Plains into the City

Because Lot never dealt with these hidden flaws, it wasn't long until Lot was drawn back into the life of sin from which he had originally been delivered.

Like a magnet that is naturally drawn to metal, something in the city pulled on the soul-strings of Lot that had never been severed, until he found himself no longer living in the plains near the city, *but living in the city itself.*

The sin of this city was so gross that fire and brimstone rained down upon the cities of Sodom and Gomorrah until there was nothing left but smoke. Even the ground collapsed and became concave on account of the judgment of God that settled in upon the plains.

Before the judgment fell, Peter tells us that God *"delivered just Lot, vexed with the filthy conversation of the wicked. . . ."* (Second Peter 2:7).

Notice Peter says that God "delivered" Lot. The word "delivered" is taken from the Greek word *ruomai* (ruo-mai), and it refers to a last ditch effort to save someone from destruction. It is the very same word used in Colossians 1:13 to depict what Jesus did for us when he "delivered us from the kingdom of darkness. . . ."

Just as Jesus saved us when we could not help or save

ourselves, God reached into the contamination of Sodom and Gomorrah and personally "snatched" Lot and his family and pulled them out of destruction.

Lot was so calloused by now, and so numbed to the voice of God, that God had to go in there and "rescue" him. Had God not done this, Lot would have perished in the holocaust that devoured the plains.

Notice what Peter calls this backslidden man of faith. In spite of the fact that he was living in the midst of the world's most wicked cities, Peter still refers to him as *"just Lot."*

The word "just" is taken from the Greek word *dikaios* (di-kai-os), and believe it or not, it refers to "righteousness."

The fact that Peter could call this backslidden man "righteous" assuredly tells us that God is able to see through the muck and deterioration of a backslidden believer's life.

If God could look at the deceived and backslidden condition of Lot, and can still call him "righteous," you can be certain that God sees beyond the sin and deception that binds any hard-hearted believer that you know. Though they appear to be far from Him in their actions, He has kept a close eye on that original commitment they made to Him years before.

This is good news for all of us!

This is especially good news for false prophets and false teachers. They may currently be involved in great deception and may be causing terrible harm to the Body of Christ; but if their original commitment was genuine, Jesus is able to see beyond their activities to the commitment they first made to Him years ago.

Yes, it is true that they are hurtful to the Body of Christ and are involved in deceptive activities of the worst kind. Still yet, if they started out with a genuine commitment to the Lord, *then they are still the Lord's.*

But notice how Peter tells us "just Lot" was living. Peter

continues to say that God *"delivered just Lot, vexed with the filthy conversation of the wicked. . . ."*

The word "vexed" is extremely important. It is taken from the Greek word *kataponeo* (ka-ta-po-ne-o). It is a compound of the words *kata* (ka-ta) and *poneo* (po-ne-o). *Kata* describes a downward motion and carries the idea of *domination*. *Poneo* means "to work."

When the two words are taken together, they denote the act of putting so much work on someone, that it results in their "total exhaustion." Thus, the word *kataponeo* ("vexed") can be translated "to wear out, to tire out, to break down" or "to bring to a place of total and complete exhaustion."

By choosing to use this word, Peter is painting a picture for us. The progression of Lot's moral and spiritual deterioration can be determined on account of this word "vexed."

Peter's usage of this word means that Lot, after having pitched his tent toward Sodom and mentally playing with sinful images that he knew were in the city, then moved into the city — *thinking that he would live near sin without participating in sin.*

However, the daily activities of the men of Sodom and Gomorrah eventually "vexed" him. Because Peter uses the word *kataponeo* to describe this "vexing" process, we know that the behavior of Sodom and Gomorrah began to "eat away" at Lot's resistance.

While he had coaxed himself into believing that he could live near sin without participating in sin, he soon discovered the power that sin possesses. The activities of the city eventually began to "wear him out, tear him down, break him down" and "totally, completely exhausted" him. Thus, in the end when his resistance was lowered, he *subcumbed* to the temptation around him.

To what degree he subcumbed to sin is not known. However, it is known that in time he became so accepted in the city, that he was promoted to a public position as an elected official.

How do we know this? Because when the angels came to destroy the city, the Bible says that "Lot sat in the gate of Sodom." To "sit in the gate of the city" was an Old Testament expression to describe those who had the rule of the city. One scholar has even speculated that Lot may have been *the mayor* of Sodom.

This indicates the level to which Lot had sunk spiritually. In order to get the vote of the people, it would have been necessary for him to stand by the needs and rights of the people. Did he adhere to the civil rights of homosexuality? We can only *speculate* at this point, but it appears that he did.

What *is* known is that Lot had wrongly thought he could live in the midst of this iniquity without becoming a part of it. Over the passing of time, the pressure of the city, combined with the hidden flaws of his life that had never been corrected, caused this "man of faith" to act no differently than the wicked residents of Sodom and Gomorrah.

Notice what primarily "vexed" Lot: *"vexed with the filthy conversation of the wicked. . . ."*

The phrase "filthy conversation" is a key to the environment that surrounded Lot. The word "filthy" is taken from the Greek word *aselgeia* (as-el-geia), which describes "unbridled living." It also carries the idea of "sensuality." The word "conversation" is from the Greek word anastrophe (a-na-strophe), and it describes a person's "lifestyle" or "behavior."

These two words, when taken together as one phrase, tell us emphatically that Lot was surrounded by "unbridled, outrageous, sensuous lifestyles and behaviors."

Even the strongest believer can be worn down by the constant onslaught of daily sinful surroundings. This is the very reason that Paul instructed Timothy, "Flee also youthful lusts. . . ." (Second Timothy 2:22).

When Sin Comes Calling

When Balaam could not successfully curse the people of God, he used another method to destroy them. He seduced them into unbridled, sensuous living by dangling the prostitutes of Moab before the men of Israel.

Numbers 25:1-3 says, "And Israel abode at Shittim, and the people began to commit whoredom with the daughters of Moab. And they (the daughters of Moab) called the people (the men of Israel) unto the sacrifices of their gods: and the people did eat, and bowed down to their gods. And Israel joined himself unto Baal-peor. . . ."

The men of Israel in this text did exactly what Lot had done to himself. They played with danger until danger finally grabbed hold of them and begin to play with them!

Notice the progression of how sin lured these Hebrew men into whoredom. *First, the daughters of Moab called unto the men.*

These were the prostitutes that served at the altar of Baal. This quite literally means that they were flaunting their near naked bodies in front of these strong, muscular men; inviting them to come and take advantage of their flesh.

Secondly, they called them into the place of sin. After tempting them sexually and flaunting their bodies directly in front of their eyes as if to offer themselves freely, they urged the men to follow them.

Whether or not these Hebrew men initially intended to commit sin is not known. It is plain, however, that these men wanted to take a closer look.

Then we come to the third step in the progression of sin. *They tasted, were tempted and and were seduced.* Once drawn into the temple where sensual activity abounded, the Bible says that *"the men did eat. . . ."*

The food to be eaten in these pagan temples was placed on the very same idolatrous altar where sexual acts occurred.

The fact that they sat down to eat really implies that they sat down "to watch." This was the equivalent to Old Testament pornography.

The temptation became so powerful that the Bible says the men *"bowed down to their gods. . . ."* Or for our fourth point, you could say *they laid their morals and convictions on the altar.*

Finally, after playing with sin, watching sin and coming closer and closer to sin, the Bible says *"Israel joined himself unto Baal-peor. . . ."* Or for our fifth point, *Israel consummated the sin that they had been mentally tempting themselves with in Moab.*

This is always the progression of sin that occurs in the life of a believer. *This was the very pattern that gripped Lot:*

1) **Sin called unto him. . . .** so he dwelled in the plains close to Sodom and Gomorrah.

2) **Sin called him to the place of sin. . . .** so he left the plains and moved into the city of Sodom itself.

3) **Sin tempted and seduced him. . . .** so he became more involved in the everyday affairs of the city.

4) **Sin vexed him. . . .** until he lost all sensitivity to the wrong that was around him and even subcumbed to it himself.

There is no doubt that Lot was conquered by the daily observance of sin, and by the hidden flaws he had never allowed God to deal with in his life.

Dwelling With the Wrong Crowd

In the event that you haven't yet caught on as to how "vexed" Lot's soul was, Peter makes his message even plainer.

He says, "For that righteous man dwelling among them, in seeing and hearing, vexed his righteous soul from day to day with their unlawful deeds. . . ." (Second Peter 2:8).

There are three key words to this verse. They are the words "dwelling," "seeing" and "hearing." According to

248

Peter, it was these three things that "vexed" Lot's righteous soul.

As we proceed to look at these three things, we must remind you for the second time that Peter calls Lot a "righteous man." The fact that he has repeated these two verses in a row, tells us explicitly that Peter is trying to make a point. Though deceived and caught in sin, Lot had not lost his "righteous" standing with God.

Why do I make such a point of this? Because in this chapter about false prophets and false teachers (Second Peter, chapter two), Peter is likening these deceived leaders to backslidden Lot.

By calling Lot "just" and "righteous," Peter lets us know that many of these deceived leaders are genuine brothers and sisters. They are just as righteous as we are; just as righteous as Lot was; but are caught in the bondage of deception.

How they were caught in this deception is obvious from the example of Lot. However, to make sure we understand how deception occurs, Peter continues.

First, Peter says that that Lot *"dwelled among them. . . ."*

The word "dwelled" is from the word *egkatoikeo* (eg-kat-oi-ke-o), and it depicts the act of "settling down into a new home and making yourself to feel comfortable there." It was used throughout New Testament times to describe "permanent residents" of a community.

Here was Lot's first drastic mistake. He chose the wrong place to live and the wrong friends to associate with. Unfortunately, he was so influenced by the wealth and prosperity of Sodom, that he was willing to lay down his godly convictions in order to have a piece of this worldly success.

Likewise, most ministers who have become false prophets or false teachers began to falter spiritually because they choose the wrong spiritual friends, associates and advisors.

Many good men and women of God have been tainted

because they listened to the wrong people. They violated their convictions and listened to advice which they knew was, shaky, in order to promote their own cause.

Attracted to the worldly success that other leaders have attained, many who started out as good men and women of God have laid their integrity on the altar in order to gain a piece of this worldly success.

Dwelling among the wrong spiritual friends is a major step to becoming a fraudulent prophet or teacher. Choose your spiritual associates carefully!

Numbing the Conscience

Peter continues to tell us more about Lot's spiritual and moral deterioration. He says, "dwelling among them, *in seeing and hearing. . . .*"

The phrase "seeing and hearing" represents Lot's next drastic mistake. The word "seeing" is taken from the Greek word *blepo* (ble-po), and it means "to look" at something. The word "hearing" is from the word *akouo* (a-kou-o), and it simply means "to hear."

Now Peter's illustration is getting more and more involved as he shows us the power of evil influences in our lives.

Statistics show that if a person watches enough violence on television, his or her sensitivity to violence will soon be *numbed*. The same statistics show that if a person watches enough pornography, though it may have deeply bothered him or her at the first, in time he or she will lose their sensitivity to how wrong this type of behavior is. They will become *numb* to it.

What we watch and hear greatly determines what we become. Lot watched and heard so much foul sin on a daily basis, that he became hardened to it; so hardened that he was able to live in the midst of it for years.

Likewise, if a young man or woman with a real call of

God on his or her life picks the wrong spiritual friends; and watches them as they do things that are spiritually wrong day after day and month after month; though he or she may have inititally been distressed by this behavior, if he or she doesn't stop listening to it and watching it, it won't be long until he or she becomes *numb* to this, too.

In fact, with the conscience *numbed* to the seriousness of this questionable behavior, he or she will probably begin to start picking up some of these attitudes and behavior themselves.

Lot made the drastic mistake of "seeing and hearing" things that were detrimental to his soul. We must guard our eyes and our ears lest we make the same mistake.

God has called us to be people of integrity, not people of compromise.

Spiritual Torture

Peter continues to tell us that "dwelling among them, in seeing and hearing, *vexed his righteous soul. . . ."*

The word "vexed" which Peter now uses is different from the word that was used before. This is the word *basanidzo* (ba-sa-nid-zo), which is usually translated "torture."

The fact that Peter would use this word tells us that the sin of the city, which conflicted with the moral beliefs that Lot had been taught, caused him great pain. It was like putting himself through continual *"torture."*

Even more, the word *basanidzo* indicates that Lot was personally doing things that caused a total violation of his whole being. What these outward actions were is not known, but the word *basanidzo* tells us that inwardly it was tearing him to pieces. He knew that he was not behaving as a righteous man should act.

I have no question concerning the mental status of Lot. By willfully engaging in activities which he knew were wrong, he stressed his mind and soul to the place of "torment." He was under an unbearable load of distress.

Lot made all the wrong decisions that he could have possibly made. He mentally played with the notion of sin; he dwelled among the wrong crowd; he saw and heard things that defiled his soul; and participated in activities which caused his entire life to be one huge episode of torture.

Lot's deception and insensitivity to sin had become so rank, that God had to literally snatch Lot from the fires of judgment.

The Lord Knows How to Deliver the Godly

How did Lot get out of this mess? Why did God deliver him? If he put himself in this position by his own free will, then why did God intervene and rescue him? Why?

Furthermore, how do false prophets and false teachers get out of their mess? If they willfully went into this deception, will God still snatch them out of it?

In light of these questions about Lot and others who are ensnared in deception, Peter joyfully declares, **"The Lord knoweth how to deliver the godly out of temptation. . . ."** (Second Peter 2:9).

Then how does He do it?

Again, Lot is our illustration in this text. Therefore, we must turn to the Old Testament to see how God delivered Lot from his predicament.

In Genesis 18:1, we find that the Lord appeared to Abraham in the plains of Mamre, and with Him were two angels.

As the conversation between Abraham, the Lord and the angels continues, the Word says, "And the men rose up from thence, and looked toward Sodom: and Abraham went with them to bring them on the way. And the Lord said, Shall I hide from Abraham that thing which I do. . . ." (Genesis 18:16-17).

As they approached the top of the mountain where they were standing, the Lord said, "Because the cry of Sodom and Gomorrah is great, and because their sin is very grievous; I will go down now, and see whether or not they have done altogether according to the cry of it, which is come unto me; and if not, I will know" (Genesis 18:20-21).

In the following verse the two men, or angels, are dispatched by the Lord into the cities of Sodom and Gomorrah to make an investigation of the sin that was there. "And the men turned their faces from thence, and went toward Sodom; *but Abraham stood yet before the Lord*" (Genesis 18:22).

Notice especially the phrase, *"but Abraham stood yet before the Lord."*

Abraham knew that the condition of Sodom was probably worse than what the cry of it had sounded like to the ears of heaven. What's more, he knew his nephew Lot was in that city along with his wife and children.

Serious Intercession Before God

It was because of his family that *"Abraham stood yet before the Lord."*

He knew that if he did not do some fast talking with the Lord, his nephew and family were going to be wiped out by one sweep of a hand as the judgment of God fell upon Sodom and Gomorrah.

Therefore, Abraham took a serious role in intercession before the Lord. The Word says, *"And Abraham drew near, and said, Wilt thou destroy the righteous with the wicked?"* (Genesis 18:23).

Notice, first of all, that the seriousness of the hour caused *"Abraham to draw near. . . ."*

When a brother or sister in the Lord is caught in a deception that will bring destruction into their lives, *this is a time for us to draw near unto God.*

In this book, we have discussed the problem of false prophets and false teachers. Now we are discussing our responsibility to help resolve this dilemma. Like Abraham drew near on behalf of Lot, we must draw near to the Lord on behalf of misguided prophets and teachers in these last days. If we make no intercession on their behalf, they may experience the horrible ramifications of judgment.

If you were in error, would you want someone to draw near to God on your behalf?

It is also interesting to note that now Abraham calls Lot "righteous." In spite of the fact that Lot had been living like the devil in Sodom, he was still righteous seed. Realizing God's faithfulness to the righteous, Abraham drew near to the Lord and began this life saving act of intercession.

Between verses 24 and 32, Abraham begins what sounds like something that would occur at a bargaining table. One by one, he began to negotiate a deal with God that would save his family from destruction. *"Peradventure there be fifty righteous within the city: wilt thou also destroy and spare not the place for the fifty righteous that are therein?"*

He continues, *"What if there are forty-five. . . What if there are forty. . . How about if you find thirty righteous in the city. . . Will you spare if there are twenty righteous therein. . . ?"*

Finally, Abraham brings the Lord down to the number ten. He says, "Oh let not the Lord be angry, and I will speak yet but this once: *Peradventure there shall be ten found there. And he said, I will not destroy it for the sake of ten"* (Genesis 18:32).

Once he heard the Lord say, "I will not destroy it for the sake of ten," Abraham knew that he had ensured the safety of his family. There were ten of them altogether that were living in Sodom.

When Abraham began this intercession with the Lord, he knew well that there were only ten righteous within the city. Knowing this, then why did he start with the number fifty when he began this work of intercession?

You must remember that Abraham was the first man of the Old Testament to walk by faith. He walked where no other man before him had walked. He may not have known to what extent he could be bold in the presence of God. Therefore, it appears from this text that he gingerly tested the waters before he dove in head first to make his real request.

The good news is that we do not need to test the waters today. We are *invited* and *encouraged* to come before God with boldness. "Let us therefore come boldly unto the throne of grace, that we may obtain mercy, and find grace to help in time of need" (Hebrews 4:16).

Under the new conditions of the New Testament, we can "make our requests known unto God" (Philippians 4:6) with no fear of being too bold!

Realizing this important fact, we must stand before the Lord, like Abraham did on Lot's behalf, and make interecession for erring prophets, teachers and believers whom we know are headed for destruction. *How dare we talk about them, and then not pray for them!*

Abraham knew judgment would fall upon Sodom and Gomorrah once the angels had finished their investigation of the cities. This is what urged him to pray. His family was there and they would be devoured in the raging fire if he did not begin to intercede

Likewise, Peter has vividly told us that God is not a respecter of persons when it comes to the issue of His steadfast justice. He judged angels that sinned; he judged the world of Noah's day; he judged Sodom and Gomorrah; and He will judge error-ridden prophets and teachers too.

If we see a leader, brother or sister that is straying off course, and perhaps is even getting into some type of falsehood, then we must open our hearts wide and make serious intercession before God. We can help change their consequences by praying for them.

Notice that once Abraham had gotten God's guarantee that the ten would be preserved, the Bible says, "And the Lord went his way, as soon as he had left communing with Abraham: and Abraham returned to his place" (Genesis 18:33).

First of all, notice that when Abraham and the Lord had completed these spiritual negotiations, "The Lord went his way. . . ."

Things were settled in the mind of God because of Abraham's prayers. There was no need for further conversation. Though He was definitely going to destroy Sodom and Gomorrah, Lot and his family were safely sealed in the supernatural protection of God now.

Also notice that the Bible says, "The Lord went his way, as soon as he had left communing wih Abraham. . . . "

Abraham had gingerly tested the waters of boldness, and negotiated with God on behalf of his family as though he was standing at some kind of bargaining table. Religion would say that this kind of prayer was assuming, forward and audacious. However, God viewed this kind of straightforward prayer as *"communion!"*

To the natural eye it *did* appear that Abraham was trying to "con" God. *"How about fifty. . . Who'll take forty-five. . . How about forty. . . What do you say about thirty. . . who'll take twenty. . . "* And finally, he brings God down to his last offer — *"ten!"*

The fact that God could call this kind of prayer "communion" plainly tells us that God loves it when His children come to Him to make straightforward demands! God was *delighted* with Abraham's intense concern and boldness in prayer.

After Abraham was finished, he too was pleased. The Bible says, "And Abraham returned unto his place."

How could he return home and resort to his regular daily routine when he knew two entire cities were going to be destroyed?

Because he had ensured the safety of his family through prayer. He could sleep in peace, knowing that God's hand would honor his righteous, but backslidden family members who were living in the cities.

What peace it brings to the soul when you know that someone else has been delivered from destruction, and now made safe, because *you* stood in the gap and prayed for them!

It was for this reason that Abraham could return home, go to bed and sleep sweetly. He knew that God would honor His requests and Lot would be preserved.

God Remembered Abraham

As the Biblical story continues, the angels arrive at Sodom to investigate the sin of the city at about early evening. Who do they find "sitting in the gate of Sodom?" Righteous Lot!

After discussing their evening plans with Lot, Lot beseeched them to come to his house for dinner that evening. It is probable that Lot did not want these angels roaming the city at night, lest they should see the sin that was there, and carrying out their instructions to destroy it.

When the men of Sodom learned that two new men were in town and were at Lot's house, the Bible says "the men of Sodom, compassed the house round, both old and young, all the people from every quarter. . . ." (Genesis 19:4).

Imagine how twisted this city must have been! These two angels looking like men had been in town for only a couple of hours, and the news of two new "men" had already traveled throughout the entire city like fire!

We know that these Sodomites had evil intentions for these two new men because the Bible says, "And they called unto Lot, and said unto him, Where are the men which came in to thee this night? Bring them out unto us, *that we may know them. . . ."* (Genesis 19:5)

As the story continues, the men of Sodom are struck with

257

a supernatural blindness by the angels — in order to momentarily save Lot and his family, and so that the men of Sodom could not find their way out of the city when the fire began to fall.

Furthermore, the angels laid hold of Lot and his family and forcibly removed them from the city before it was consumed.

Did Lot want to leave? *No.* Did the angels make him leave? *Yes.* If Lot didn't really believe judgment was going to fall (see Genesis 19:16), and lingered there as long as he could, then why did God rescue him?

Genesis 19:29 says, "And it came to pass, when God destroyed the cities of the plain, *that God remembered Abraham,* and sent Lot out of the midst of the overthrow, when he overthrew the cities in the which Lot dwelt."

In other words, God didn't save Lot for Lot's sake — *he saved Lot for Abraham's sake.*

Had it been left up to Lot, Lot would have been consumed in the iniquity of the city. He himself was too twisted and seared to know that he needed to be delivered. Therefore, it was for Abraham's sake that Lot was delivered. *Because of Abraham's intercession, God delivered and preserved this backslidden, yet still "righteous man."*

Will God Remember You?

Can it be said that God has held back His judgment upon someone else because of *your* prayers and intercession?

We must make it our goal to pray for those whom we know are caught in deception.

Like Lot, these individuals may be so deceived that they are unaware of how critical their situation really is. If it is left up to them, they will probably continue in their same course of action, and thus, experience *divine retribution.*

Thank God that we can help make a difference on their behalf!

The Word says, **"The Lord knoweth how to deliver the godly out of temptation."** *How does He do it?*

He does it through the intercession of the saints who are willing to stand in the gap on behalf of others who do not know to pray for themselves. By standing in the gap and making intercession for these error-ridden individuals, many have been spared and brought back into a place of restoration and usefulness once again.

As we come now to the close of this book, this must be our own response to this problem within the Church in these last days.

We must develop discernment about false prophets and false teachers, but we must also go to our knees in prayer to see them rescued and set back on a right path.

If you had thought of certain individual as you have read this book, then take Abraham's example and go to your knees. Pray for them.

God may deliver them for *your* sake, dear friend!

If you were caught in deception, wouldn't you want others to do this for you? You can make a difference in the lives of other people!

ENDNOTES

Endnote numbers 1-7 are taken from *The Story of Lucy and Stigmata Blood* by C. B. Roberts on the following pages: 5,9,12-16.

Other Books by Rick Renner

Dream Thieves
Dressed to Kill
Living in the Combat Zone
Seducing Spirits and Doctrines of Demons
The Point of No Return
The Dynamic Duo
Spiritual Weapons To Defeat the Enemy

Additional copies of this book and other book titles
from **ALBURY PUBLISHING** are
available at your local bookstore.

ALBURY PUBLISHING
Tulsa, Oklahoma

For a complete list of our titles,
visit us at our website:
www.alburypublishing.com

For international and Canadian orders,
please contact:

Access Sales International
2448 East 81st Street
Suite 4900
Tulsa, Oklahoma 74137
Phone 918-523-5590   Fax 918-496-2822